Advance Praise

"What a script: The head of a disaster institute, who trains others on emergency response, discovers he has Stage 4 cancer, putting to the test everything he has taught. Jaime Aten blends together what he has learned from disasters, both large and small, and offers practical suggestions that can equip all of us to prepare for our personal trials."

—PHILIP YANCEY, author of *Where Is God When It Hurts?*

"Sooner or later we're all smacked by the great storms of life. Whether hurricanes or illness or divorce or death, it's hard to know what to do and how to respond. Drawing on rich research and personal storytelling, Dr. Jamie Aten provides an inspiring and practical resource to get you through. Don't miss this gem of a book. "

—MARGARET FEINBERG, author of *Fight Back With Joy*

"Jamie's vulnerability in sharing the raw reality of his 'personal disaster'—being diagnosed with Stage 4 cancer at age 35, a young father of three girls—will be a balm to anyone who has experienced a disaster of their own. There are no empty promises or inspirational clichés here. Through his personal story and his expertise gathered through years of disaster research, he finds meaning in the struggle and continually comes back to the powerful, enduring promise of God's faithfulness to redeem our suffering."

—ED STETZER, Billy Graham Distinguished Chair, Wheaton College

"This beautiful book perfectly marries vulnerable personal narrative with professional expertise. The result is a work that leaves a lasting impression and one you will go back to over and over for reference. Aten pulls us in and carries us along as he paves a clear path for all who need to maneuver through .our own personal disasters."

—SHAYNE MOORE, author & director of operations
at One Million Thumbprints, NFP

"Dr. Jamie Aten has crafted something special here. Through the lens of his own local suffering, Aten simultaneously takes readers on a global journey—reminding us all that though we are irrecoverably marked by our pain, we are also united by it. Where there is suffering, there is authentic resilience. And where there is resilience, there is hope. Reader, dive in and allow *A Walking Disaster* to gift you with its hard-won, authentic hope."

—AUBREY SAMPSON, church planter, speaker, and author
of *The Louder Song: Listening for Hope in the Midst of Lament*

"*A Walking Disaster* is a compelling personal story, woven with psychological and sociological research, and at the same time instructive in healthy responses to both natural and personal disasters. This book is timeless, written in the tone of humility, and deserves a long shelf life."

—JO ANNE LYON, general superintendent emerita and
ambassador of the Wesleyan Church

"Dr. Aten has written a moving, honest, and inspirational memoir that will give hope to anyone seeking to recover physically, psychologically, and spiritually from a personal disaster. As a scientist and a Christian, rooted in his family and his community, Aten delivers a fully human account of enduring a period of immense suffering and emerging on the other side, fragile but intact, with a new conception of his life, his work, and his faith. Highly recommended."

—HAROLD G. KOENIG, MD, professor of Psychiatry & Behavioral Sciences, Duke University, and codirector of Duke's Center for Spirituality, Theology and Health

"Jamie tells his story with vulnerability and humor, weaving in relevant research with gems of insight from the faith. I couldn't put this book down. This book is a powerful model of the redemptive meaning the Christian faith brings to even the worst of disasters."

—M. ELIZABETH LEWIS HALL, PhD, professor, Rosemead School of Psychology and associate editor, *Psychology of Religion and Spirituality*

"This is a book for everyone. Why? Because nobody is immune to the jolts of life. And that's why I urge you to read this compelling book by Jamie Aten. It's grounded, practical and powerful. Every page will inspire you. Don't miss out on this powerful message."

—LES PARROTT, PhD, #1 *New York Times* bestselling author of *You're Stronger Than You Think*

"Jamie Aten has written a beautifully human book, endowed with the superhuman strength of hope. Fiercely honest, he makes navigating impossible circumstances possible, breathing courage into not only those of us working to mitigate conflict, disaster and human suffering, but also into those of us who are experiencing our own painful life disasters. I walked away from this book changed, and profoundly grateful."

—BELINDA BAUMAN, executive director,
One Million Thumbprints

"Dr. Aten writes with a holy charge, telling his survival story with cancer in a gripping manner. What is unique about this account is the comparison of his personal disaster with mass disasters that are happening worldwide. This book is a must read for disaster response practitioners who want to 'get'er' done', alerting us to the emotional and spiritual toll disaster survivors go through."

—KEVIN KING, executive director,
Mennonite Disaster Service

"Many people feel compassion for and respond to disasters. Few study them. And even fewer commit themselves to teaching others how best to care for men, women, and children during and in the aftermath of unexpected trauma. Dr. Jamie Aten is one of those few. His insights, both from working in disaster zones and from an unexpected encounter with early-life cancer, are deep, nuanced, and profoundly spiritual. If you are looking for wisdom on how to engage disasters—both personal and communal—there may be no finer book. I can't recommend *A Walking Disaster* highly enough."

—KEN WYTSMA, author of *Pursuing Justice*
and *The Myth of Equality*

A Walking Disaster

A
WALKING
DISASTER

WHAT SURVIVING KATRINA AND CANCER
TAUGHT ME ABOUT FAITH AND
RESILIENCE

Jamie Aten, PhD

TEMPLETON PRESS

Templeton Press
300 Conshohocken State Road, Suite 500
West Conshohocken, PA 19428
www.templetonpress.org

A Walking Disaster is a work of nonfiction. While all the stories
in this book are true, some names and identifying details
have been changed to protect the privacy of the people
involved.
Set in ITC Stone Informal by Gopa & Ted2, Inc.

Library of Congress Control Number: 2018959566
ISBN: 978-1-59947-544-8 (cloth: alk. paper)

This paper meets the requirements of
ANSI/NISO Z39.48-1992 (Permanence of Paper).
A catalogue record for this book is available from the
Library of Congress.

18 19 20 21 22 10 9 8 7 6 5 4 3 2 1

Printed in the United States of America.

With all of my love to my wife Kelly
and daughters Colleen, Chloe, and Carlee.
I am so grateful and thankful
for each of you.

Contents

Preface

S QUINTING TO KEEP swirling sand out of my eyes, I stepped out of the batter's box. Proudly sporting a red jersey that boasted the logo of our rural Little League sponsor, Riker State Farm, I took a practice swing while imagining sending the ball over the back fence. Glancing toward the bleachers, I saw parents huddled, chatting in small groups.

Their concerned faces told me something was wrong.

The evening had begun like any other warm June evening, but out of nowhere the winds had picked up and the sky had turned black, glowing with a strange greenish haze.

When adult volunteers flagged us to return to the dugout, I glanced over my shoulder to see the coaches huddled with umpires around the pitcher's mound. As I reached my own parents among all the family members waiting to receive their players, I heard the ump yell, "Game called due to weather," waving his arms toward the parking lot for everyone to leave the ballpark. Car doors were already slamming shut as fans without children playing quickly packed up and headed for safety.

The suddenness of the emergency exit was frightening.

The moment my family walked in the front door of our gray split-level home, among the southeastern Illinois cornfields in the town of Oblong, my parents hustled my younger brother, Travis, and me down to the basement. Passing through the living room, my mom grabbed some baseball cards to distract my brother and me from the looming storm. In the basement, my parents flipped over the navy couch where we'd play video games and instructed my brother and me to crawl under it.

We'd been in the basement for about five minutes when the phone rang, and my father picked it up. Hearing the howling winds getting louder, I looked up from reading Ken Griffey Jr.'s stats on the back of the Upper Deck baseball card in my hands to see my father's brow furrow and the corners of his mouth turn downward.

Hanging up the phone, he announced, "Aunt Kathy called to say a tornado had been sighted just two miles north of here."

We were staying burrowed down in our makeshift bunker.

A few minutes later, the lights cut out. Clicking on the flashlight my dad kept beside his workbench, we listened to a transistor radio, waiting for word that the storm had passed.

Eventually, through a slim window facing our backyard, we saw the sky begin to lighten. My dad ventured out first and spotted a tornado in the woods just a mile from our house. Although he could see objects flying through the air at its base, he heard only silence. After watching the tornado ascend toward and then beyond the clouds, he allowed us all to venture outside.

Curious, we all jumped in our old black Dodge truck, lined up four across on the hot, sticky, tan vinyl bench seat, and headed toward the area where the tornado had touched down. Peering outside, wishing the truck had air conditioning, my brother and I could see that the twister's trail of destruction, destroying some things and missing others, had been entirely arbitrary.

Although our family, our home, and our land had been unscathed, we later learned that parts of the nearby town of Newton had been leveled by the two-hundred-mile-per-hour twister. In fact, in the subdivision where my aunt Kathy's brother lived, a dress—a flimsy cotton dress—had sliced right through a wooden door by sheer force of the wind. From Newton, the twister traveled toward us, later touching down in Oblong.

In the wake of that local disaster, I internalized the idea that when disaster came, I could hunker down, weather the storm, and throw open the storm doors to a sunny sky, resuming the same life that had been interrupted.

Years later, after completing a PhD in counseling psychology; marrying my wife, Kelly; and welcoming our first daughter, Colleen, my family moved to southern Mississippi. We unloaded our boxes just six days prior to Hurricane Katrina's arrival.

My family and I were some of the lucky ones, fleeing before the worst happened and returning to find our own home mostly intact. But as I traveled back to splintered trees and leveled houses, I was gripped by the way survivors continued to live in the wake of Katrina, especially in terms of their spiritual resources. I threw myself into researching the ways that religion and spirituality served, and in some cases did not serve, survivors of disasters. Over the next five years, I'd go on to research, train, and assist in the aftermath of numerous regional disasters and started consulting on some international projects. Later I took an endowed chair in clinical psychology at Wheaton College, and by the beginning of my second semester, I'd founded the country's first faith-based academic disaster research center: the Humanitarian Disaster Institute at Wheaton College.

All of this shaped disaster into something I studied and responded to rather than something I experienced. Outside of my research, my life felt like it was finally falling into place. Adding Chloe and Carlee, my wife and I were now the parents of three redheaded, unique, flourishing girls. Kelly was getting ready to pursue a graduate degree in nurse midwifery while working for a local midwifery practice. And I was doing what I loved vocationally, building the institute and expanding its capacity to conduct research and programs to help congregations and communities prepare and care for people in a disaster-filled world.

But disaster didn't stay within the confines of my research. The summer before beginning my third academic year, the stomach pain began. When I visited my primary care doctor, he referred me to a specialist who dismissed my concern and sent me home to take some fiber, instructing me to come back if the symptoms worsened. The symptoms did diminish for a period, but a year later the pain resurfaced, and I began experiencing a sharp discomfort in my pelvis and recurring shooting pain in my legs. I returned to my doctor, who immediately ordered several tests.

What I thought was going to be a fairly routine office visit to the doctor and minor health issue turned out to ultimately be a diagnosis of Stage IV colon cancer. At the age of thirty-five, life as I knew it came to a screeching halt.

My struggle against cancer brought tests and more tests.

Radiation.

Chemo.

Surgery.

Disfigurement.

More chemo.

Loneliness.

Spiritual struggle.

Despair.

When I was forcefully inaugurated into the cancer club, of which no one wants to be a member, I ceased to be the researcher collecting data, nodding pastorally with a clipboard in hand, or providing outreach trainings. Suddenly I was at ground zero as the unwelcome storm blew up the life I'd been living, like the crushing tornado that had ripped through Newton.

And that's where my story begins.

I invite you to share my journey with the hope that you might discover what I did. Though I never would have chosen it, what I learned along the journey that threatened my life ultimately reshaped my soul.

A Walking Disaster

Evacuation Impossible

My Body Was Ground Zero

FOR WEEKS, I'd been experiencing sharp pains that shot down my legs. I thought maybe I had a pinched nerve in my back. The pain wasn't going away, and I started to experience discomfort in my pelvic area and often felt sick to my stomach. I was hoping to get some resolution about what was wrong.

The doctor who'd performed a colonoscopy earlier in the week had assured me, right before I was knocked out for the procedure, that the chances of cancer in someone of my age and health were less than 1 percent. Because I was a young guy without any previous health issues, those odds sounded about right to me. We'd isolate the problem, treat it, and I'd be able to get back up to full speed, personally and professionally.

Married ten years, I was the thirty-five-year-old father of three young girls. It was the end of my second year on the faculty of Wheaton College, and I was energetic about heading the school's new Humanitarian Disaster Institute I founded. My wife, Kelly, was about to begin working toward her master's degree in nurse midwifery, and life in the Aten household was moving along at full throttle. My fatigue and pain, unwelcome intruders, would soon be in our rearview mirror.

Yet as I began to emerge from the fog of the anesthesia following my procedure, I heard the doctor who'd just performed my colonoscopy informing Kelly that he'd found cancer.

"Cancer?" I interrupted, only to fall back into unconsciousness.

Again and again I would fall back under the spell of the anesthesia, momentarily, only to reawaken and interrupt the doctor trying to finish breaking the bad news to Kelly. Seven times in a row I startled awake, not remembering what I had just heard, and ask, *"Cancer?"* Though I only have a memory of hearing "cancer" once, Kelly shared the absurd routine with me later.

Even if I'd been more lucid, the drug-induced routine was a telling expression of my mental state. I felt like Bill Murray in the movie *Groundhog Day*, reliving the same day ad nauseam, had it been a horror flick. Whether groggy or sharp-witted, I simply did not have a category for the information I was receiving. Hadn't the wildly unlikely odds the doctor had shared meant that I'd be fine? Rare, unfortunate disaster befell other people, not me. And yet, in that moment, my plans for my life went out the window.

Yes, I was a goal-oriented Type-A person who'd carefully mapped out the future I saw for myself. But imagining a future in which we are not afflicted by disaster or crises isn't the sole property of advance planners. The author of Proverbs 19:21 announces, "Many are the plans in a person's heart, but it is the LORD's purpose that prevails." Though it's natural to expect a future free of the unexpected, it necessarily means we are unprepared for the inevitable crises we will face. David Entwistle, a friend and colleague of mine, conducts an exercise with his students where he asks them to imagine their lives five, ten, twenty-five, and fifty years into the future. He told me once, "No one has ever talked about being divorced, widowed, having Alzheimer's, having cancer, or even just being feeble." He added, "Bad things happen, and they will happen to each of us. But by and large, we neither expect this nor plan for this." He was right. I had intellectually understood the statistics about people who would be forced to face hurricanes, tornadoes, fires, and even colon cancer, and yet I was—as we all are—completely unprepared for the unexpected. We are so bad at estimating risk that the experts have named our response the "ostrich effect." Burying our heads in the sand, we mistakenly ignore real potential threats.

The doctor referred me to an oncologist to further interpret the results. The following day, as Kelly drove me to the cancer center at Central DuPage Hospital Cancer Center to meet with Dr. Patel, I was nauseous and felt a shooting pain in my pelvis.

I had no family history of cancer. The worst health problem I ever faced was a broken bone in my hand, in fifth grade, from playing basketball. A million questions swirled through my mind as we pulled into the hospital parking lot. Kelly drove around the lot awhile before scoring a spot just a hundred yards from the front entrance of the cancer center.

Each step between the car and the door were heavy with the weight of the unknown.

A greeter at the information desk had pointed us in the direction of Dr. Patel's office. We'd set out as if we'd understood, but as we got farther from her desk, signs reading "Oncology," "Infusion," and "Radiology" all began to blur together.

When we finally found our way to the oncologist's office, we stood at the receptionist's desk waiting to be checked in.

"Can I help you?" she asked.

I looked away when she leaned over her desk to make eye contact.

"What's your name?" she continued.

"Jamie Aten," I said tentatively, as if unsure of whether I wanted to be him.

Still trying to make eye contact with me, the receptionist asked, "Why are you here?"

I'd not expected the question.

"Umm . . . ," I stammered, searching my mental Rolodex for the newest words in my daily vocabulary. "Cancer" or "tumor"? "Pelvis" or "colon" or "rectum"?

I chose against "cancer," as if speaking it aloud would afford it more power. I also steered away from both the broad "pelvis" and overly specific "rectum."

"They found a tumor in my colon."

The word caught in my throat, and I felt a welling behind my eyes.

"Alright," she replied, glancing up at me and handing me a clipboard. "Fill out your health history and then bring it back to me."

I went to reach for the clipboard but my arm and hand fell numb by my side. After a second, I started to reach for it again with my shaky arm. After a gentle glimpse and slight reassuring smile that started at the corner of her mouth, Kelly stepped in and took the clipboard for me.

Turning to scan the room, Kelly and I beelined toward the last pair of available seats.

A full year before I was diagnosed, I had visited a specialist for the pelvic and stomach discomfort I'd been experiencing. His advice? "You're so young, don't worry about it. You just need more fiber in your diet." Because of my age, he'd overlooked the possibility—granted, a slim one—that my symptoms could signal something more serious. So he sent me home with some packets of dissolvable fiber to stir into water from time to time. The prescription provided some relief. When the symptoms returned, accompanied by shooting pain in my legs and pelvic region, my general practitioner suggested a CT scan and colonoscopy. The CT scan revealed a mass resting on a nerve bundle. Had it not been for the shooting pains in my legs, I may never had known I had cancer.

I scanned the magazine rack beside the water cooler, searching for any worthy distraction. The magazine that I

selected seemed promising until, flipping through it, I realized that, although there were some helpful articles, it was
like one big marketing ad for pharmaceutical companies.

CALLED

"Mr. Aten?"

A nurse technician wearing brown scrubs called my
name, and Kelly and I rose to follow her. We ducked into a
small room where she measured and recorded my height
and weight.

In a sterile treatment room, much more disappointing
than the colorful room at my daughters' pediatrician's
office, I sat down beside Kelly.

"I need you up here on the table," the nurse instructed,
pointing to the paper-covered treatment table.

I considered not complying but dutifully climbed up and
sat down. She clamped my finger with a device to measure
my heart rate and squeezed my arm with a Velcro blood
pressure cuff.

"Hmm . . . ," she sighed after announcing my blood pressure numbers. I knew they were high for me.

"Are you stressed?"

Was anyone coming for a diagnosis *not* stressed?

"Yeah, I am," I confirmed.

Scribbling in my chart, she let me know the doctor would
be in soon. As she left the room and closed the door, I heard
her drop the chart into the plastic holder on the outside of
the door.

Defiantly, I returned to my chosen chair.

As Kelly sat beside me, I had a feeling of déjà vu. Though I'd never sat in an oncologist's office, the moment felt eerily familiar.

It hit me.

Nine years earlier I'd been teaching as an assistant professor of counseling psychology at the University of Southern Mississippi in Hattiesburg, a little over an hour from the Mississippi coast, just two hours from New Orleans, when Katrina was sweeping across the Gulf of Mexico heading toward land.

Kelly and I, having moved with our then two-year-old daughter, Colleen, just six days earlier, had been visiting a local Southern Baptist church in Hattiesburg when the pastor announced that a storm was headed toward the coast. A seasoned local, he assumed that most folks would go home, batten down the hatches, and weather the storm as they'd done so many times before.

Because our new home was in the country, we couldn't get a TV signal. Cable was scheduled to be installed the next day. The cell carrier we'd used in Chicago had poor reception where we now lived, so we'd not been in touch with family and friends. And though I'd met some of my work colleagues, I had no idea how to reach any of them if they weren't on campus. So, when the pastor announced that Katrina was heading our way, the news was coming as a surprise to me.

If this had been a tornado, like I grew up with in the Midwest, I'd have known to go to the basement. But there were few basements where we lived because of the water table. As soon as the church service ended, I asked a woman sitting behind me if we should be worried.

With confidence she assured us, "At worst it will be like camping for a day or two."

As Kelly and I mulled around after the service, chatting with folks in the church, the prevailing opinion was that the storm would pass without incident. These folks had been warned of storms in the past. They'd hunkered down, weathered the storm, and made it out on the other side relatively unscathed.

My thoughts took a personal turn. I wanted to believe that what I was facing would be of the "camping weekend" variety of cancer. I still wanted to believe that I could escape the impending storm.

After that church service in Mississippi, without phone or Internet, Kelly, Colleen, and I went to my office to check my work computer for weather reports. With Colleen on my lap, we waited for a weather map to load. Though we were new, what we saw was concerning. The hurricane was headed straight for Hattiesburg.

I felt completely helpless.

Unable to anticipate what was headed our way, we decided we didn't want our daughter experiencing unnecessary trauma if we could avoid it. We kept asking ourselves, "Are we overreacting?" Ultimately unable to answer that question, we decided to evacuate. Time would tell.

Kelly and I dashed home to pack up some essentials for our family before fleeing. As we drove toward our new home, with most of our belongings still unpacked, I remembered all the post-9/11 public service ads that stressed how one common household item was crucial to everyone's preparedness kit. As soon as we got home, I started rummaging through our drawers and unopened boxes to look for this lifesaving resource. Then I found it. The holy grail of preparedness, or so I thought: duct tape!

I was standing in the living room looking out our window, gripping that duct tape. I knew a threat was rapidly approaching, but all I could think was, *Now what?* I was in over my head. Nothing had prepared me for the devastation that was about to rip through our community.

I dropped the duct tape on the floor, packed up some keepsakes and belongings in our tiny silver Saturn four-door, and headed out of town with my family. Traffic on 59 North was thick, but it wasn't yet stalled the way it would be just a few hours later. Once we were out of the city, we just started calling friends. Ryan and Kristen, the closest friends who picked up the phone first, lived in Nashville, about six hours away, and were happy to receive us. If the storm blew over as the pastor suggested it most likely would, we'd spend the night, drive back on Monday, and have a story to tell our friends in the Midwest about the adventure of living in the South.

When we woke up the next morning in Nashville, the television showed that Hurricane Katrina had struck the Gulf Coast in the early morning hours. Stretching four hundred miles across, the storm's winds were 100 to 140 miles per hour.

The pastor was wrong.

We saw on the news that Katrina was still a Category 2 hurricane when it hit Hattiesburg with sustained winds around 100 miles per hour. It looked like bombs had been set off from the coast well past our new community. Debris was everywhere. Pine trees pierced homes like missiles. Concrete slabs were all that some people could point to that remained of their homes.

As Kelly and I waited for Dr. Patel, I felt the same helpless feeling I'd felt nine years earlier.

Wearing a white coat, stethoscope hanging from his neck, a well-dressed, slender man of average height walked into the room where Kelly and I were waiting.

"Hi, I'm Dr. Patel."

Kelly and I stood to shake his hand and then we all sat down. I knew from the first glance he was all business.

He spun his chair around, signed into the desktop computer, and clicked into a folder that contained my scans.

The screen filled with images from my previous scans, tests, staging procedure, and colonoscopy. "Here's the mass in your pelvis sitting on the nerve bundle the CT scan found before," he narrated.

Then tracing a path from the mass with his ink pen he pointed to the tumor in my colon, "It's cancer" he said.

I felt like I was back in my box-stacked office, eight years earlier, looking at radar images of Hurricane Katrina heading for our home.

Dr. Patel continued, "It's advanced. We think the cancer started with the tumor in your colon spread to create the mass in your pelvis," he said matter-of-factly. "From this it appears you have Stage IV cancer."

As his words hung seemingly hung in the air he added, "But the results from the first biopsy were inconclusive so we will need to perform another one after your surgery to officially confirm your staging."

"But the mass could still be benign, right?" I pleaded.

"Well . . . it could be . . . but the fact that you have a tumor and this mass, we think it's metastasized," he uttered.

Dr. Patel went on, "I also want to take a full body scan to learn more, to see if the cancer has possibly spread elsewhere in your body."

His words collided against one another in my head. In retrospect I realized that it felt like the state the narrator in *The Great Gatsby* described when he said, "I was both within and without at the same time." I was at once overwhelmed by what I was learning and, at the same time, almost felt myself floating away from my body and what I was experiencing.

He kept speaking awful words like "aggressive" and "advanced" and "late stage." Unable to piece them together into a coherent whole, I knew I could trust that Kelly, an experienced nurse, was catching them. There would be more tests, he explained, and then we'd determine a plan of action.

Detached from what was happening in the room, I began to tear up. Though I tried to will myself to hold it together, I felt myself coming unglued.

As if my tears were the prompt Dr. Patel needed to be

reminded of my humanity, he realized that he couldn't keep talking. He paused to offer me space to gather myself.

"Jamie, maybe we pause here," he suggested. "Tell me what it is that you do."

His posture softened, and his force field of professionalism dissipated. He was still all about business, but I recognized the air of warmth that signals an effective caregiver.

"I'm a professor at Wheaton College. And I run a disaster research center."

I watched his face as he processed what I'd just said.

After considering my answer for just a moment, he replied, "You're in for your own personal kind of disaster."

My head jerked up and I looked him in the eye. Feelings of anxiety, helplessness, sadness, confusion, and shock were calmed for a moment. The synapses in my brain began firing as if they'd been lit by a flare from the emergency preparedness kit stored in my basement. Though I still couldn't process all the words he'd been using, his reframing of my situation as a disaster would later set the stage for how I thought about my cancer experience. I now had a box with which I could organize my experience.

I understood disasters.

There will be chaos.

This means I'm in the impact phase.

I'm in shock.

Hold it together.

Remember what you've seen others survive.

There are road maps for response and recovery.

For a brief moment, Dr. Patel naming what I was facing

as a personal disaster lifted me out of my shock and anxiety by offering me a familiar context as a lifeline. I knew how to prepare for and respond to tornadoes, hurricanes, earthquakes, and other mass traumas. But cancer? The feelings of helplessness and anxiety that had overwhelmed me during Katrina came flooding right back with a spike of intensity.

He asked a few more questions and then gently guided us back to the scheduling desk to make our next appointment.

"I've ordered another scan for you downstairs in a couple days," he explained.

"But I already had a scan before they did the colonoscopy," I protested, fearfully. I felt like a child who'd had a nasty run-in with a dog who was then gun-shy thereafter when encountering any dog.

"Yes, but this time we'll do a PET scan with dye. If there is any cancer that's spread, it should light up and we'll be able to see it."

Spread? It hadn't yet occurred to me that cancer could be floating through my body.

"This will give us some more information to help us know how to treat you."

He stood before he finished the final sentence.

I knew he was speaking to me, because I could see his mouth moving. I heard his voice but struggled to process the words. It was this absurd doctor's office scene where the adults speak with great concern and all Charlie Brown hears is, "Wah wah wah cancer wah wah wah."

I was Charlie Brown.

"When the results come back from the scan," he promised, "we'll develop a plan."

Had I been able to form words, I would have blurted out the racing thoughts bumping up against each other in my mind. *"Plan?" What does that mean? Chemo? Surgery? How much time do I have?*

I shook his hand and then he walked briskly out of the room. Kelly and I tried to retrace the path back out to the receptionist's desk.

As Kelly and I drove home in silence, I reflected on Dr. Patel's diagnosis and why, given the signs and symptoms, it had still come as such a devastating surprise to me. There were lots of reasons, of course. There were my natural human defenses, protecting me from what I was not yet ready to face like my inherent optimistic bent.

Survivors often describe life as life before and life after a disaster. A post-Katrina cartoon I'd seen in the Jackson, Mississippi, newspaper showed a timeline demarcating B. K., "Before Katrina," and A. K., "After Katrina." As a goal-oriented person, the trajectory I'd planned for my life had suddenly been severed in two: "Before Cancer" and "After Cancer." I had no idea how long the second segment would last.

Frozen in pure, helpless disbelief, with no idea where to turn or what to do, I wanted only to wake up from the nightmare over which I had no control. More than anything, I wanted to grab some duct tape, hop in our minivan, and flee the disaster that was coming whether I liked it or not.

But this time, there was nowhere to run. Disaster wasn't striking someone else, somewhere else. It hadn't ruptured open the sky above me or shaken the ground beneath me.

My body was ground zero.

CHAPTER 2

Don't Be an SUV

When Helpers Make It Worse

T WO DAYS after my appointment with Dr. Patel, I found myself back at the cancer center, being called into a wide room where I would receive my PET scan. Kelly was asked to wait outside, and I was asked to take off any clothing with metal. I laid my glasses on a table and stowed my shoes, the left one holding my wedding ring, underneath.

Wearing track pants and a T-shirt, I wandered out toward the ominous, large white machine.

A kind nurse in blue scrubs queried, "Would you like a blanket?"

"No, thank you," I replied without thinking. "I'm fine."

I was anything but fine.

Realizing a little warmth sounded comforting, I retracted my refusal. "Wait, yes I would. I'd like a blanket."

Reaching into a cabinet, she handed me a carefully folded blanket. I wrapped it around my middle and sat down in a chair against the wall.

"This is how it'll work," she began.

Without Kelly at my side I knew I needed to concentrate on the nurse's instructions. I was rattled when she described the injection of dye I'd receive. I was already in physical pain and braced for impact. I'd not yet recovered from the week's internal poking and prodding, and every new person I met wanted to do more of it. I now intimately understood white-coat syndrome, in which people experience a fear of doctors, to the point that it changes their vital signs.

I was afraid to get the scan. Afraid they'd find the cancer had spread. Afraid I'd receive a death sentence.

After the nurse prepared the needle, she had to remind me to keep breathing. As I looked away from the nurse, she counted to three and injected a vein in my forearm with the dye. Trying to focus on regulating my breathing, I attempted to focus on some cherished memories, like our family playing outside at a park with my daughters' laughter filling the air.

After the injection was complete, the nurse helped me up onto the PET scan machine. She made friendly chitchat as she helped get me situated. She left when the technician enterd the room.

The tech, dressed in brown scrubs and a black jacket, was a woman who looked to be in her fifties. Her blonde hair was pulled back in a ponytail. She helped me lie down, positioning my abdomen at just the right spot, guiding me to stretch my hands over my head as the bed I was lying on began to slowly inch toward the small white cave.

She assured me, "We'll slide you in, and the machine will let you know when you should take a deep breath."

The tech added, "Okay, now I'll stand out of the way, but I'll be watching the test on this screen."

She pointed to a screen that looked like Dr. Patel's desktop screen.

"And when it's over, will you tell me what you see?" I asked, eager for more information.

Dutifully she replied, "That's for the doctor to go over with you."

Though I wanted to protest, I knew there was no point. Hospital policy was what it was. But I secretly figured that if she could see the test, her face would reveal her reaction. Or, I reasoned, perhaps to throw off savvy patients like me, her affect would go completely flat. But knowing I'd be expecting her to show no affect, maybe she'd force a reaction other than the natural one. Like Vizzini and the man in black in *The Princess Bride*, my thoughts bounced back and forth again in my head.

Catching myself, realizing the futility of trying to discern her expression, I mentally reminded myself, *Don't go there. Don't look at her face.*

When she stepped away, I felt the machine begin to move my body slowly toward the white cave.

"Stay still," the voice from beyond coached. "Keep breathing but be prepared to hold your breath when we tell you."

In that vulnerable moment, the image of my girls' faces flooded my consciousness. That's when I realized: *I have to tell my girls that Daddy has cancer.* When they returned from their grandparents' place at the end of the weekend, we'd have to tell them. With that single thought, picturing their innocent faces, something gave way inside me and my body began to quiver.

No matter how much I tried to stop, my shoulders kept shaking. It wasn't a polite little cry, either. It was deep, heaving, ugly sobbing, and I couldn't stop.

The nurse stopped the belt that had been loading me into the cave.

In no hurry at all, this woman I'd known for all of ten minutes gently placed her hand on my left shoulder.

It was a sacred moment.

My brain hadn't been able to stay locked in practitioner mode. And though I tried to excise the thought of my precious girls, just to get through the scan, I couldn't shake the picture of their faces and the horrible lot of telling them. Once we told them, their innocence would be shattered. Whether I survived cancer or succumbed to it, their lives would be irrevocably altered by the possibility that their father could die.

My body continued to shake, more of a mild tremor.

Slowly removing her hand from my shoulder, the tech made eye contact.

"What's wrong?" she asked gently.

"I've been diagnosed with cancer," I explained, "and I just fell apart when I realized I have to tell my girls that Daddy has cancer." I sniffed at the end, as a concluding punctuation.

Quietly she queried, "Do you think you can finish?"

"Yeah, I'll try," I promised. "I think I can do it."

The fact that she'd been able to meet me right where I was, connecting in such a deep way, had helped me. I made a mental note to tell my psychology students how helpful the appropriate touch and patient listening had been for me.

I'd always taught my students that, when warranted and invited, effective listening would be useful in their practice as well. I'd assure them that most people want to help but don't know how—and that being present to another's suffering, physically, emotionally, and spiritually, is what those in crisis need most. Although a lot of people feel like they need to have all the "right" answers before they can help, people who are hurting need relationship itself more than they need certain words. One of the greatest gifts someone can offer is to listen well and be present to another's suffering. That means demonstrating warmth and concern while turning off the part of your brain that's paying more attention to what you're thinking than to what's being said. In some cases, letting another know that you hear and grasp the gravity of what they've been through might even mean crying with the other person.

We'd practice this when I'd taken students out in the field after a natural disaster. When engaging with women and men whose lives had been devastated by flood, fire, or hurricane, my students' impulse—their natural human impulse—was to do something to *fix* the situation. And while there's definitely a place for lacing up work boots and hauling away debris, other volunteers could do that. What I most wanted my students to learn was how to listen well to those experiencing disaster and to be a steadfast loving presence to those whose lives felt so completely untethered.

When this radiology technician had patiently and gently touched my shoulder, averting her eyes but letting me know she was present with me, she had done exactly what I wanted my students to do as they interacted with people in crisis.

Then the tide turned.

Before resuming the process, the tech administering my scan turned her face fully toward mine and remarked, "You know, Jamie, God only tests the strong."

Wait, what?

Did she really just say that? Did I hear it correctly?

Her surety that the ill that had befallen me had been sent by God's hand was a flagrant spiritual violation. However, having worked in disaster contexts for so long, I knew she was just trying to help. While it was a wildly inappropriate thing to say to a patient, I tried to let it go.

My "helper," though, did not move on.

She continued, "At least you're not going to have it as bad as I did. I was a mom and I was *single.*"

Is she really comparing her experience to mine in this moment?

On one hand, I understood that she was anxious and didn't know what to say. On the other hand, I knew, as a fellow helping professional, that what she'd done was insensitive and harmful. As an act of self-care, I knew I needed to distance myself from her remarks.

"I think maybe just give me a minute," I asked.

My mind was reeling. For years I'd used Steve Corbett and Brian Fikkert's *When Helping Hurts* to teach my students about "helpers" who, though they often mean well, end up causing more hurt than help. Months after Katrina, I attended a large community gathering of leaders held at the Biloxi Coliseum to discuss disaster mental health needs. We were gathered around circle tables throughout a large meeting room and you barely could hear the speakers up front because of the conversation and chatter at each table. Then a woman entered the room from a door toward the back far left side of this giant meeting area, and silence began to fall at each table she passed. Tension in the room increased with every step she took. When a few people shouted some jeers at her, I wrestled to figure out what was happening. Then she took a seat just a couple tables away in an empty spot. When she turned around to take off her jacket and place it on a chair, I understood why people were angry. She was wearing an official blue jacket with the four-letter "F" word in bright yellow letters: FEMA. The agency's initial lack of response hurt a lot of people, and I saw in that room the anger and bitterness that lingered in the hearts of those who'd been affected and in the region. Though the agency would learn from its mistakes and would move forward to help so many, hearts in the room were still raw.

Feeling particularly vulnerable in my thin hospital gown and thin blanket, I was completely dumbfounded and shocked. *Did she really just say that!?!,* I thought to myself. What could have been harmful quickly turned into an almost humorous moment in my disbelief: *Well, now I have the perfect example the next time I train others in trauma care on what not to say in a crisis.* I gave the tech the benefit of the doubt that she was just trying to help. But then I reflected that I couldn't have been the only vulnerable patient who'd been subject to such comments. I wondered what they might have felt if she shared similar sentiments. Had her words felt no less brutal—and personal—to other patients than the initial lackluster efforts of FEMA had to Gulf Coast residents? I'd seen so many people, like this tech, whose hearts were in the right places end up causing harm to disaster survivors.

Eventually, I made it through the scan.

After the scan, as I tied my shoes and slid my wedding ring back on, I continued to seethe about the counter-lesson I'd just learned.

Helpers who aren't helpful is a common theme in the disaster world, especially spontaneous unaffiliated volunteers, whom many emergency managers simply refer to as "SUVs." This isn't neighbor helping neighbor. Instead this refers to people who parachute in on their own accord or send unrequested and unhelpful resources.

In 1989 the *Exxon Valdez* oil tanker struck a reef in Alaskan waters and spilled almost 11 million gallons of crude oil into the waters, impacting fish and other wildlife. While the event had a devastating impact on the environment and economy, people were not displaced from their homes. And yet, in response, volunteers sent an influx of donated clothing to the area. Included in the shipments were barrels and barrels of swimsuits. Sent to Alaska. In the winter. Helpers aren't always helpful.

After Hurricane Katrina in 2005, one church in the northern United States raised sixty thousand dollars to purchase frozen microwavable meals for disaster victims without access to power to cook the meals. The well-meaning folks filled a semi with the meals and sent it to southern Mississippi. Without any way to refrigerate the meals, they eventually rotted on the side of the road. Helpers aren't always helpful.

And in 2012, when twenty children and six adults were slain at Sandy Hook Elementary School, a nation feeling helpless to alleviate a community's suffering began sending a huge number of letters, cards, toys, and other gifts that overwhelmed the community's ability to manage them. The town of just twenty-seven thousand residents received over sixty-five thousand teddy bears! So, the energy of responders and volunteers had to be used to store and ship stuffed animals rather than helping those who were hurting. Helpers aren't always helpful.

Unfortunately, the medical technician's insensitive comment wouldn't be the only response that added to my suffering rather than relieving it during that season. Some of those around me offered similar trite platitudes as the tech had. Others whom I had expected to support me after learning of my diagnosis withdrew from me and my family. I now understood intimately that even helpers wearing navy jackets with bright yellow letters could, and would from time to time, fail.

By necessity, my health and physical well-being became front and center in those earliest days. In time, though, I knew that a healthy recovery would demand that I tend to the garden of my heart as well. Our research on the survivors of the Liberian genocide pointed to the necessity of forgiveness for long-term recovery. Both the huge, gut-wrenching forgiveness required of those survivors and the smaller, offense-releasing forgiveness that was my lot were important ingredients in a recipe for recovery. And while a *speedy* pardon isn't always useful, effective, or even possible, attempting to forgive early on lays the groundwork for future health and wellness.

Like much of what I'd discover on my journey, implementing best practices while weathering a disaster was easier said than done.

Sheltering in Place

Seeking Refuge in God

A s I CONTINUED to go through tests and felt more and more disconnected from any normalcy in my body, I found I was also struggling to find normalcy in my relationship to God. My understanding of faith has shifted throughout my life, but cancer unsettled me—and opened me—in ways I hadn't imagined.

My faith journey began in a rural farming community in Oblong, Illinois, where I grew up among cornfields in a town whose population hovered around one thousand people. My decision to be baptized at a Sunday night church service, at age eight, was an emotional one, a response to a deep, soulful inner prompting.

A decade later, while I was considering what my next step would be after high school, I attended Lincoln Trail Community College—also situated in the middle of cornfields, about twenty-five minutes from where my family lived. There my faith began to shift from being rooted in emotion to being more intellectually grounded.

One unlikely source of spiritual guidance came from an English professor during that first year of college. John Makosky was like no one I'd ever met in Oblong, or anywhere for that matter. He was a poet, he read philosophy, and he had lived the life of a vagabond. Some days he was agnostic, and on others he seemed to embrace Eastern spirituality. Yet, like Dorothy touching back down on her grandparents' farm, John Makosky landed in a world where even those who didn't practice the teachings of Jesus identified as Christian. I noticed this as a ten-year-old, when I heard women in a local diner gossiping about a friend's sister, home from college, who was dating a boy who didn't believe in God. The listeners gasped in unison at the scandalous announcement. Boy, John would have really given them a run for their money! And for whatever reason, he took an interest in me, and even introduced me to genres of jazz I had never heard before.

One day John—who requested his students use his first name—asked me to see him after class. I had no idea what he wanted to discuss.

After the other students had filed out, I approached his desk.

"Jamie," he asked, "are you a Christian?"

"Yes," I answered, unsure where our conversation was heading.

His next question was one I'd never been asked before.

"Why?" he queried.

I was stumped. Because I'd been raised in church and had been active in my church's youth group, I knew that I

believed in God at a heart level, but I was unable to articulate the intellectual reasons I believed in God.

My professor didn't press further, but I left his classroom
that day with his simple question bullying my head and
heart.

Why did I believe in God?

When I got back home, still rattled, the first thing I
did was call the youth minister from my church. He had
invested in my life for years, and I trusted that he could
help.

I quickly steered our conversation to the real reason I'd
called.

"Brad," I admitted, "I don't know why I'm a Christian."

"Okay . . . ," he offered, mulling over my question. "Did
something happen to make you ask this?"

I explained about my professor's question.

He asked, "Have you heard of *Mere Christianity*?"

"It sounds familiar, but I haven't read it," I answered.

"It's a book by an author named C. S. Lewis—"

"Oh," I chimed in, "Narnia, right?"

"Yes," Brad confirmed, "same guy. *Mere Christianity* is
a Christian apologetic, kind of an explanation for faith,
from some radio talks Lewis gave during World War II, and
I think it'll be helpful to you as you try to answer the why
question about your faith."

The next day I stopped by church and picked up the book
from Brad. Ignoring my class assignments, I devoured it. I
had never heard or read anyone like Lewis. *Mere Christianity* opened my eyes to a whole new way of seeing my faith.

Growing up, I had absorbed messages from some Christians that education and intellect were likely to threaten one's faith, but Lewis' words awoke a part of me that I didn't know was there. Most of my life to that point I would say I knew God largely through rules—rigid lists of dos and don'ts. I had never read a book from cover to cover, other than picture books as a kid. But with every page, every idea, Lewis opened my eyes to see and start to understand God in a whole new way. I couldn't stop reading. It was like listening to the sheets of sound on John Coltrane's *Giant Steps* album that John Makosky had lent me. Everything I thought I knew about jazz had changed. So it was with my faith; it expanded and soared to new heights when I read Lewis.

After I finished *Mere Christianity*, my youth minister mentor suggested another book, then another, then another. After one of our visits, I left his office precariously walking to my truck balancing books from my waist to my chin.

As John and I continued to discuss the divergent ways we each viewed the world, he suggested one day, "Why don't you bring me a book from your perspective? And I'll give you one."

Feeling more confident, I agreed, and brought him *Mere Christianity* the next day. When I dropped it on his desk, John pulled a book from his desk drawer by some Eastern yogi and handed it to me. Our cadence continued like Art Blakey and Clifford Brown swapping jazz solos as we continued to meet weekly and discuss what we were reading.

If it was possible to be mentored in the Christian faith by an agnostic, I was!

As I was growing up, I'd felt God in my heart. And then, in college, I had this rich opportunity to know God in a more intellectual way. After a year of junior college, I transferred to Indiana State University where I majored in psychology. I got a job as a part-time youth minister and continued to burn through books by authors like Augustine and Tolstoy and every C. S. Lewis book I could get my hands on.

Indiana State University was ten times the population of Oblong. The first week of school, when other students complained that there was nothing to do, I thought they were being sarcastic.

"I can't believe all there is to do is go to the movie theater," grumbled one student.

Really feeling like I'd landed in the big city, I chimed in, "It's so cool that there's a movie theater in *this* town!"

Shortly after arriving on campus, I volunteered and worked in two different research labs. Throwing myself into my studies in a way I never had, I was drawn to the writings of William James and Gordon Allport, who were among the first to study the psychology of religion. While searching for a book in the mildew-smelling basement of the school library, I stumbled upon the *Journal of Psychology and Theology* research journals. Reaching for one of the volumes, bound with orange tape, I brushed dust off the cover and inhaled old-book smell when I cracked it open. I'd found my new happy place. That I could know God more deeply intellectually through science only fueled my intellectual curiosity.

In addition to robust new conversations with other students at this secular institution, a campus minister named Mark Gallagher took me under his wing. In many ways he was the Christian version of what John Makosky had been to me—minus the agnostic-hipster-antiauthority-counterculture vibe. We got together every week, often at a Tex-Mex restaurant called Tumbleweed, for what we called lunch and the question of the day. Over chips and salsa, I'd share with Mark what I was learning in one of my classes or the insight I was noodling on from a theology book I'd picked up from the local used bookstore. I'd then share a question or idea I'd been trying to understand in more depth or sometimes to just get my head around a topic. Mark's thoughtful responses and queries opened my eyes to a deeper life of the mind as a Christian.

I'd gone from being the boy who was asking his father if Jesus would care if we played baseball in the backyard on my baptism day to the young adult who was consuming books on theology, church history, and Christian living. I was convinced that God existed, that God had come into the world in the person of Jesus Christ, and that God was still actively engaged with our world.

But if I'm honest, in my twenties and early thirties, I almost never felt God's presence; my relationship with God was more about facts than faith.

Sure, during certain moving songs in worship I'd feel the

life-giving breath of God's Spirit, but this had only happened a time or two. Or when people would share a powerful testimony of God's work in their life, I could recognize
God's nearness to those who trust him. I envied friends who
worshiped at churches where they felt connected to God.
As an adult with undiagnosed Attention-Deficit Hyper-
activity Disorder (ADHD)-inattentive type until the age of
thirty-two, I could give myself to prayer and worship, but
it often felt hard for me to be still enough in my mind to
really experience God's presence in a visceral way. But if I
consumed enough caffeine, I'd experienced—what I'd later
find out is called "hyperfocus"—an ability to intensely zone
in on God through study. So in adulthood, my primary
experience of God was more of an intellectual awareness
than an emotional experience of God's presence.

Cancer changed that experience for me. I felt so physically tortured and mentally foggy that I couldn't rely on
my intellectual theological thoughts. My primary mode of
feeling close to God was cut off by my present condition.

Two weeks after my diagnosis, I began medical leave
from work. Always exhausted, I was hunkered down at
home, leaving only for medical appointments. Kelly and
I had planned to attend the American Psychological Asso-
ciation Convention in Hawaii, which would have been our
first time there, and were disappointed to have to cancel
that trip.

At the end of my first week at home, I had to go to my
office to retrieve some documents I needed as I attempted
to keep juggling work responsibilities. Hoping everyone

would be out of the office at lunchtime, I snuck in right after noon.

True to form, our amazing office coordinator, Linda, was still at her desk. She kept everything running smoothly in the department at the Humanitarian Disaster Institute. I knew her to be a faithful, godly woman.

"Hi, Linda," I said as I entered the office. "I shouldn't be here but needed to grab a few things."

"Jamie," she quietly said, standing from her chair to give me a hug, "it's so good to see you."

Receiving the warm gesture, I thanked her and ducked into my office. Gathering everything I thought I could possibly need during my stay at home, I left my office and began to walk past Linda's desk again.

"I have something for you," she announced, holding out a package wrapped in flowery wrapping paper.

"Awww," I answered, receiving the gift, "thank you, Linda. Thank you so much. I'm so grateful."

Already exhausted from the short drive to school and my office pillage, I didn't have the energy to pause to open the gift. Gathering it up with the rest of my load, I took it with me and headed toward the elevator.

Linda called out after me, "Don't worry about anything here. We've got it covered!"

By the time I got home, I had to use the last of my strength to walk from the driveway into the house. Dropping the files in my first-floor office, I carried Linda's present upstairs with me so that, if I never made it back downstairs, I wouldn't lose track of it. Dropping it beside my nightstand, I fell into the bed and was asleep in a matter of moments.

When I awoke two hours later, the girls were still at school and Kelly was at work. As I slowly became alert, I reached down beside the bed and picked up Linda's gift. Tearing off the paper, I found what looked like a bright teal-blue blanket.

Odd, since it's the end of July . . .

Unsure of what I was looking at, I unfolded a note that had fallen out of the package when I removed the paper.

"This is a prayer shawl," Linda had penned. "When you wear it, it reminds you of the presence of God."

I knew that Linda was a knitter, and felt so touched that she'd lovingly, and prayerfully, knit me this shawl. Since I'd been ill and been so uncomfortable, we'd thrown caution to the wind and were blasting our air conditioner at full throttle. Propping up a few pillows against our headboard, I hauled myself up into a sitting position to pray.

Unfolding the shawl, I draped it over my head, shoulders, and back. I'd already resigned myself to being unable to pray long, beautiful, or eloquent prayers, so I purposed only to pray one word: *mercy.* Inviting the Holy Spirit to translate those two simple syllables to God's ears, the intention of my heart was to ask God for mercy on me, mercy on my children, mercy on my wife. Although I had no idea what form that would take, that was my prayer.

After a few minutes of sitting upright, I felt a shooting pain in my back. Letting gravity have its way, I rolled over to lay back down on the bed in the fetal position. Tugging at the prayer shawl, I used it to cover my body. And when I'd prayed the word "mercy" so many times that it began to lose meaning, I could still feel the slight pressure of the shawl on my skin.

Overwhelmed with physical pain, anxiety, and uncertainty, I couldn't have the kind of emotional experience of God that I'd enjoyed in my youth. And, far too overwhelmed and exhausted to study Scripture, stand in church for more than a few minutes, or concentrate in prayer, I struggled to connect to God spiritually. Intellectually, I was having difficulty finishing sentences, let alone entertaining coherent thoughts about God.

And yet, somehow, during the minutes and hours when that prayer shawl was draped over me, I felt like I didn't have to depend on either my heart's emotion or my head's knowledge to encounter God. It was actually one of the few times in my life when those two were joined in what I can only describe as God's presence. The weight of that prayer shawl, enough to feel but not so heavy that it was uncomfortable, ministered God's real presence to me. In the moment, I almost felt God's embrace in that knitted yarn, like a hug. And on most days, when my words failed, the most I could do was simply be still in God's presence under that shawl.

I'd spent so much of my life either running after God or running from God. Growing up I'd been shaped by a somewhat legalistic faith that saw the world as black-and-white. I believed I had to earn God's love. Later, I'd intellectualize the immeasurable transaction that happened between God and humanity. But the consequence of my illness was that I discovered I only needed to be still before God. When I had no more strength to run or perform, I was finally still enough to experience God's nearness with me. On my sickbed, under that prayer shawl, I was able to lean into God.

Another kindred spirit, in ministry and in walking with those impacted by disaster, also tasted God's closeness in the midst of suffering. After serving as a canon at Coventry Cathedral, in Coventry, West Midlands, England, Andrew White moved to Baghdad to become an Anglican chaplain in Iraq. Serving the only Anglican church in Iraq, White was affectionately nicknamed the "vicar of Baghdad." In his work as president of the Foundation for Relief and Reconciliation in the Middle East, White served refugees who fled their countries due to violence and war. We were excited to have him share his experiences with the students in our research lab at the institute.

In their devastation, when they were most vulnerable, Rev. Canon Andrew White cared for those who had lost everything. In a situation in which many would be tempted to despair, he offered the living hope of God's real presence.

"The Lord is here," he promised. "His spirit is with us. When you have lost everything, Jesus is all that's left." He went on to describe the terror that had occurred under the rule of Saddam Hussein and after his ousting. But he also shared how God can redeem places of suffering. He added, "We would eventually worship in the very place Saddam had ordered out crimes against humanity and turned his pool into a baptismal."

Rev. White, living with multiple sclerosis, understood suffering as an opportunity to experience the real presence of Christ. He knew intimately not only that God is present when we suffer but also that those who suffer are afforded a unique opportunity to experience refuge in God.

I want to affirm that, without romanticizing suffering in any way, I believe that refugees exiled from their homes, clergy people afflicted with disabling disease, and bed-bound professors ravaged and debilitated by cancer all have access to the God who suffered.

In the middle of the day, when I was restless and could find no physical comforts, I noticed God's presence, which was as close as my prayer shawl. And in the middle of the night, when I was sleepless and unable to find physical comforts, I felt God's presence, which was as near as the blankets Kelly had pulled over me before she'd joined me in bed.

In my darkest days, God ceased to be either an emotional feeling or a heady idea. When I needed God most, God became real in a very tangible way.

Crisis Communication 101

Honoring Your Whole Story

" **I**T'S GOOD we caught it early."

The words continued to ring in my ears long after I hung up the phone with my parents. They'd known I'd been feeling sick and was having tests, and I'd called to fill them in on what Kelly and I had learned at my appointment.

It's good we caught it early.

After the odd words escaped my lips, I *heard* them. Realizing what I had just uttered, after seeing the surprised look on Kelly's face, I corrected myself, confirming that we actually *didn't* catch it early. Later, as I mentally reviewed our conversation, I could hear the way the buoyant words exposed my resistance to the new reality that had been thrust upon me. Upon *us*. I hadn't meant to misrepresent my situation to my parents. The only person I was lying to was myself. A part of me believed that attempting to shield others from the reality of my disaster would, in some magical way, enable me to withstand the pain. My reaction, ignoring the signs of a real potential threat, was a painfully cliché textbook expression of the ostrich effect.

All the book learning in the world didn't make my gut responses to disaster any different from any other sufferer who hadn't completed a PhD in counseling psychology or spent a career researching disasters.

In the twelve years we'd been married, Kelly had—in all things, and not just medical matters—been the realist and I the optimist. Though I was typically unrepentant, we both knew that my impulse had always been to try and turn the negative into a positive. With her signature mama-bear strength, she offered, "We really need to be careful that you don't say that we caught it early when we tell the girls."

She was right. The way the news of an impending or recent disaster is shared matters deeply to those who receive it. Picture the local public official who's been charged with preparing a community for an impending disaster standing behind a podium in front of an official-looking blue backdrop. If the messenger overestimates the severity of an event, the community spends inordinate time and money and energy preparing for it. When they eventually discover that "it's not that bad," they lose faith in the message and the messenger. And if the messenger minimizes the expected impact and the community experiences something far worse, the community is ill-prepared to face what's coming. As we anticipated sharing with our girls, my temptation to defend myself, by minimizing the event for others, gave way to a new desire: I wanted to do right by my girls, who depended on Kelly and me to equip them to weather the storm.

Kelly and I both knew that the way in which we'd narrate the event for the girls would either equip them to access all the resources they needed to face the storm that was coming or it would lull them into believing that it would pass without doing lasting damage. And that wasn't a promise we could make. Though I had no interest in discussing it, Kelly and I both carried the heavy awareness that she might be parenting our three girls alone. In that awful eventuality, the way we chose to tell our girls about my cancer mattered deeply. And my training did convince me that Kelly's bent toward realism would serve our daughters better than my tendency to focus on the positive and avoid the negative. In that way, she was our strong anchor. Without her, I might not have had the courage to be real with our daughters and may have repeated the ruse I'd tried on my folks.

Although I intellectually believed in the value of brave truth-telling, the shift in my personal practice was harder won.

"I want to reassure them," I told Kelly. "I want to let them know that we've got this."

Kelly challenged, "We can let them know that, as the adults, we're handling it, but we want to make sure we don't inadvertently lie to them about how serious it is."

Though we'd discussed whether we'd tell the girls one by one or together, we decided that we wanted to have the conversation together as a family. But because of the girls' various developmental stages, as well as their wildly diverse wirings and temperaments, deciding how to word the news was a pretty unwieldy situation.

Everything in me wanted to be the calm, competent official who could put everyone else at ease as he steered the ship. But the reality I was being forced to face was that I wasn't *just* the messenger who announced the impending disaster. I was the vulnerable person in harm's way—if the person in harm's way was chained to ground zero with absolutely no escape contingency. In the earliest days after my diagnosis, though, I desperately wanted to be the person in charge of organizing help. It's a role on which I'd constructed my identity. But the disaster I was facing was too big and had already hit too hard. Whether I liked it or not, I was the person getting walloped by the storm who was in desperate need of disaster assistance.

Bittersweet Homecoming

The day after I spoke to my folks, Kelly's parents drove Colleen back home after spending the week with them. We got a lot of snuggles in that day and let her settle back into being home, listening to the girls swap stories to play catch-up on the week's events.

After we'd cleaned the kitchen following dinner, Kelly's parents excused themselves to go on a walk and we invited the girls into the living room, letting them know we wanted to discuss something serious. Kelly sat down on the couch, and Colleen, who was ten, curled up in an overstuffed chair next to it. I was sitting on the floor and Chloe and Carlee, then seven and four, joined me. The older girls' faces revealed that they sensed something was wrong.

When we were all settled, Kelly began by describing my symptoms, "Dad's been having some pains."

Carlee was our spunky, happy-go-lucky child—petite, with a head full of red curls. While Carlee wasn't old enough to catch the full meaning of her mom's words, a glance at Colleen and Chloe told me they were clearly grasping the gravity of the situation. They knew this wasn't the stomach flu.

I told the girls that I had something called "cancer," describing where it was located and that it had spread.

Seven-year-old Chloe was the first one with a question, chirping, "What's cancer?"

Chloe is our extrovert, a social butterfly. No—not butterfly—more like social hawk. Truly, she is a force of nature. Tall for her age, her physical strength was matched by a strong personality.

Kelly offered, "It means some lumps are growing inside Daddy's body that shouldn't be there so the doctors are going to give him medicine and an operation to try and get rid of them."

"And the fact that it spread," I interjected, "actually helped us know that it was there. If it hadn't reached and touched something that's called a nerve bundle, I might not have felt it for a while and it might have gotten worse."

Clearly, releasing the impulse to force the positive, for myself and others, would be an ongoing process.

Our oldest daughter, Colleen, was gentle, introverted,

smart, and her dry humor was already starting to bloom. She tended to pick up on things most other kids her age wouldn't think of. Her concern?

"Is it contagious?"

Kelly explained that cancer was not contagious, and we did our best to answer the rest of the questions each girl asked.

On paper, Kelly and I, a nurse and a psychologist, would appear to have a handle on every skill set needed to navigate this conversation with our daughters. And had we been having it with someone else's children, in a hospital waiting room or a private-practice office, we could certainly help someone else's children understand a situation like this one. But in that room we weren't the objective professionals we wished we might have been. While we chose not to burden the girls with details like life expectancy—less than three years for a diagnosis like mine—the very real possibility that our babies could be fatherless before Colleen reached high school hung in the air between us. No amount of optimism could erase the grim reality.

We had been talking for about thirty minutes, though it felt like an eternity, when four-year-old Carlee raised her hand like she'd recently learned to do in preschool.

When I nodded for her to ask her question, she queried, "Why do we have pink soap in the bathroom downstairs, and why does it smell like strawberries?"

All four of us burst out laughing, followed by Carlee laughing at our laughter. I had to wipe tears away because

I laughed so hard. That moment of innocence was exactly what we all needed.

After the girls asked a few more questions, we assured them that we loved them, that Daddy had good doctors, and that we were doing everything we could to fight the disease. We closed by praying together, asking God to be our helper and provider.

That night, before Kelly and I turned out the light in our bedroom, we agreed that we'd done what we'd intended to do.

TRUTH TOLD

Concerned about the pain and fear it could cause, I'd been terrified to share with my girls the reality of my cancer diagnosis—both for me and for them. But, with help from Kelly, I'd realized that I owed my girls a realistic picture of the struggles ahead.

If I'd operated the way I always had, by downplaying the severity of the situation, I would have done more harm to everyone. We were careful to never promise that I was going to be okay or beat cancer. Though convenient in the moment, minimizing what we were facing would have made our family's journey more difficult in the months to come. Instead we focused on letting them know we were going to do everything we could to try and overcome cancer.

Though I'd never made the personal connection to my

own tendency to put a positive spin on reality, I'd seen officials—who could predict that a disaster *might* take a dangerous turn—withhold information to avoid inciting fear. The result, though, when the event took a turn for the worse was that more harm was inflicted because the population was unprepared.

Giving our girls the most accurate version of the story we could offer, in a way that was developmentally appropriate for them, served them well, and it also served us. And when I failed to have the strength be realistic with our daughters, Kelly kept us on track.

But many curious others would not be privy to this kind of honest telling.

In the past, mental health professionals used an intervention called "critical incident debriefing" immediately after disasters. The idea was that if we could get people together to tell their stories right after a major tragedy, we could prevent them from experiencing long-term trauma. We now know, through emerging research, that, at best, this approach is not helpful; at its worst, it can be quite harmful. Sometimes we need to hold on to our stories for a time so we can properly cope with them. I *didn't* choose to unpack the intimate details of my story with every student and colleague I passed on campus. Sharing trauma before we are ready is like volunteering to have a wound opened when no supplies are available for bandaging the injury. Because of this, I shared sound bites of my experience with people outside of my family and close friends.

Sometimes these sound bites were optimistic. Sometimes they were not.

While I recognize that I didn't have to tell the whole story to everyone I knew, pain made it hard for me to be an accurate reporter. This was further complicated by concerns about how the news would impact our girls. I also didn't want to make others worry about me. I wrestled against my bent toward optimism in the face of my hard-to-swallow diagnosis. This was further complicated by the fact that I struggled to face my dismal Stage IV diagnosis, let alone come to grips with it. I was barely able to say and hear the word "cancer." I'd get upset whenever those closest to me used "Stage IV" language, even shutting down some of those conversations. I found myself living daily between the two poles of blind optimism and morbid despair, between faith and fear.

Being honest with the girls, though, provided a sturdy foundation for what lay ahead. And although I didn't realize it at the time, it was preparing all of us to receive what our community was about to offer.

CHAPTER 5

The President Visits Ground Zero

Why We Need Community

HELPING, along with researching best practices for helping others amid disasters, was a major part of the identity that I'd constructed for myself. I'd not only chosen a helping profession for my life's work, but within the field I'd even focused on helping those with the most desperate needs. Even in many of my other roles—as husband, father, psychologist, professor, researcher, director—I was most comfortable on the giving rather than the receiving end of helping.

After a morning pre-op visit at the hospital, I'd used all my energy to climb the stairs and crash in my bed.

"Jamie, wake up."

It was my mom's voice. She and my father had come up from southern Illinois to support our family in the weeks before my surgery. It was a Monday, and I was well into my chemo and radiation, and doing the smallest things exhausted me.

"Jamie," she spoke, "the president is here." Again she said, "Jamie wake up, the president is here."

When the president of the United States visits a disaster zone, you know it's serious. Groggy and disoriented from being in a deep sleep, I couldn't make sense of who was at our home. *Was I dreaming? Had I misheard her? Was she making a joke I wasn't understanding?* I understood that it couldn't possibly be Barack Obama, then president of the United States waiting for me downstairs in my living room, but my mother's serious tone conveyed a sense of urgency.

"What?" I asked. "What are you saying?"

"The president," she reiterated. "The president of the college is here to see you."

Okay, now that made a lot more sense.

My mom shuffled back downstairs to talk with Wheaton College's president, Philip Ryken, until I could get my wits about me.

I struggled to sit up, wincing as a shooting pain stabbed my back. I'd not changed out of my clothes from being out in the morning, so at least I was mostly dressed. Sliding on brown slippers my girls had gotten me for Father's Day, I gently eased out of bed and headed downstairs.

My mom and Dr. Ryken were chatting as they stood in our foyer.

"Hi, Phil," I said, "thank you so much for stopping by."

I eased myself down the stairs to join them.

"Of course," he answered. "You've been on my mind."

His eyes were warm and sincere with genuine concern. He asked how Kelly and the girls were doing. He let me know that many were praying for me. Then he wanted to know how I was weathering the storm.

"There are a lot of people who've rallied around us," I explained, "but I think the hardest thing for me is being the person who needs help." I went on to explain the shift from being the helper to the helpee. He nodded with a pastoral understanding.

Whether I wanted to be that person or not, the choice was clearly no longer up to me. My body had betrayed me. I could no longer put on a happy mask and soldier through the pain.

President Ryken received my admission with grace. I could read the compassion in his face. But he also offered a word of wisdom.

"Jamie, we're *all* the type of people who need help."

I nodded thoughtfully, as if allowing the words to water my parched places. As a psychological professional, I knew intellectually that what he was saying was true. As a follower of Jesus, I knew spiritually that his words were true. But in that moment, I was still resisting the abruptly undeniable reality that I was now the person who needed help.

Our visit concluded with President Ryken placing his hand on my shoulder while he prayed. He was mirroring what I'd done for so many other sufferers in my role as a youth minister, a disaster psychologist, a relief worker, and a friend.

Maybe I had enough grit to do this on my own.

I didn't want my wife to view me as weak. I didn't want my girls to see me sick. I didn't want colleagues I respected to view me as less capable. I didn't want students to question my skills. I didn't want neighbors asking me what was wrong. If there was any way for me to navigate this disaster on my own, without involving others, I wanted to do it.

When Hurricane Gustav was threatening to pound the Mississippi coast and our community, Kelly and I drove upstate to meet her parents and drop off the girls, who would spend time with their grandparents in Indiana. After we turned around to return home, I noticed that the other side of the interstate was bumper-to-bumper traffic, all cars of those who were evacuating. That's when it hit me that we were among the few vehicles, alongside the occasional emergency response vehicle, that were headed back toward the approaching disaster.

My work required me to return. As part of a grant I'd been awarded, we had trained local clergy to respond to disasters. A colleague of mine was in the safety of the emergency operations center, and if the storm hit he'd take orders from the local emergency manger and relay them to me on the ground, where I would organize the response of churches. Thankfully, the storm died out and was minor. Five years before my own disaster, I had been the person willingly heading into the storm. When the disaster was mine, however, I was forced to face the unpleasant reality that I was the one whom others were going to be rushing in to help.

A few days after Dr. Ryken's visit, I began a rigorous regimen of chemo and radiation. I was taking oral chemo pills two times a day, once in the morning and once before bed. I had radiation at the cancer center in the middle of the day. This was my daily routine, Mondays through Fridays, for three months. The label on the chemo pills warned, "Don't put in contact with skin." And yet I was expected to *swallow* that poison?

Not only was Kelly a full-time mom with a part-time job, she was also our family's FEMA administrator. She was responsible for organizing all the helpers who wanted to offer food, childcare, transportation for the kids, rides to appointments for me, and all kinds of other help. The logistics of all those arrangements were like a constantly moving 3-D jigsaw puzzle. But she didn't just arrange help, she provided more help than she asked for from others.

For Kelly, one of the important needs to be filled was finding someone to drive me to chemo because we didn't want the girls to have to go while they were home for summer break. Because I wanted to drive myself, we had some negotiating to do. And because we were jamming this important conversation into the moments before whisking the girls out the door to swim lessons, we were both busy helping to gather hair clips and towels and sunblock as we hashed it out.

"I don't need anyone to drive me," I announced, breezing past the mudroom in search of Chloe's flip-flops, "because I'm just fine."

No sooner had I finished my pronouncement than I ran into the door to the mudroom and fell over. I was so fatigued that I often lost my balance. Kelly was very gracious not to laugh out loud, though the moment was humorous, but my little spill did win her the argument.

Okay, maybe I do need a little help.

The admission was wildly humbling.

In a study of humanitarian aid leaders, we learned that humility helped those we interviewed garner a more accurate understanding and view of themselves, the people on their team, and their organization. Humanitarian aid leaders with higher levels of humility also appeared more open to collaborating and coordinating their efforts and responses to emergencies with others. The majority interviewed talked about experiences, sometimes in the field, that came close to shattering or had shattered their confidence. Swallowing their pride taught them the importance of sharing not only their strengths but also their weakness with others they counted on. We found humility has an important role to play in effective disaster response.

These humanitarian aid leaders helped me see that humility is essential to organizing successful aid. Now cancer was teaching me that humility is also essential to successfully *receiving* aid.

After the 3/11 disaster in Japan, my colleagues and I partnered with World Relief, the Japanese Evangelical Aliance, and other local Non-governmental Organizations (NGOs) to respond to those in need. Enough time had passed that large machinery had been mobilized to clear away the devastating rubble. In one community we visited, a massive yellow bulldozer was scooping and relocating huge piles of debris. One elderly survivor in an adjacent neighborhood confided in a local pastor with whom we partnered, "Every time you come to visit and listen, you remove a piece of rubble from my heart." The image gripped me. Her words were particularly poignant since I knew that accepting help was difficult in a culture where receiving any gift had to be reciprocated by offering a gift in return.

The Japanese culture, I realized, wasn't so different from that of the American Midwest in which I'd been raised. After the Great Plains Tornadoes of 1913, many of my stoic blue-collar predecessors, even those on the verge of death, proudly turned away the assistance offered to them. Also a culture in which doing for one's self was prized over receiving aid from others, one sick midwestern mother cradling an ill child had to be physically removed from her home and taken to a relief center. Another mother trying to dry a waterlogged mattress declined the offer for a new mattress, insisting that because so much had been done for them already she didn't want to accept more help.

Clearly I'd come by my stubborn self-reliance honestly. I had managed my life very carefully so that I didn't have to depend on others. And when life got difficult, I wanted to isolate and withdraw and weather the storm alone. I wanted to hide my need. I didn't want to be seen during the worst thing I'd ever endure.

But daily I was reminded that I stood, metaphorically, with the urban poor in Louisiana who didn't have the resources to evacuate. I was like the frail elderly person in inner-city New Orleans who, stranded in his wheelchair, had been evacuated by volunteers. I didn't even have the resources to pretend as if I was someone who didn't need help.

For days after his visit, Philip Ryken's words continued to

echo in my ears: *Jamie, we're all the type of people who need help*. Yes, I could admit it reluctantly. We're all mortal and we all stand in need of God's gracious deliverance.

I was afraid of having an experience similar to one of the pastors I interviewed for a study after Katrina. He described how people from his denomination came to help, but that he struggled because he felt like the patient at the hospital around whom doctors, nurses, and residents gathered to gawk, exclaiming, "Hey, you gotta see this!" Thankfully, that wasn't my experience. Those, like President Ryken, who came to visit me never made me feel like I was an oddity to be pitied. Instead, they communicated love and care.

I saw examples of pity on campus when someone would smile when passing me and then whisper something quietly to a companion.

I recognized pity on the faces of a few folks in church.

And there was no hiding my need when my friend and psych department colleague, Ward, helped brace my weight so that I could walk around my neighborhood when I was too weak to walk on my own.

Walking into a doorway and falling to the ground was just a small snapshot of my larger neediness.

Unlike the standard-issue human need with which we all live, my particular neediness couldn't be concealed. My need was exposed.

When I interviewed former FEMA administrator, Craig Fugate, he described the "whole community" approach to emergency management that benefits communities. He explained, "It's a recognition that the bigger the disaster, the more likely the first assistance is really coming from your neighbors. He added, "The people who will naturally be helping their neighbors and looking for a way to support their community. If that's how a community works day to day, why do we expect it to change when there's a disaster? . . . Church members don't have to be told to go help somebody in the congregation. We're not individuals; we're part of a bigger family. Even if we're not physically related, we still come to each other's assistance when we're needed."

Whole-community response was exactly what I experienced. Despite my stubborn pride, people from whom I'd prefer to hide my need began showing up day after day.

Kelly was always there when I needed her and shouldered the load of my needs.

My girls helped in each of their own ways: Carlee with snuggles, Chloe by drawing me pictures, and Colleen by sharing what she was reading.

Our parents would visit and help however they could.

One evening, when I couldn't stand in the kitchen longer than the time it took to quickly fill a cup of water, a woman on staff at Wheaton brought over a beautiful nutritious dinner, still piping hot from the oven.

Some of Kelly's friends helped by driving our girls to and from school when Kelly drove me to doctors' appointments or to treatments.

My colleagues and students from the Psychology Department drove me to many of my doctors' appointments, carefully avoiding bumps and potholes that sent pain through my weak frame.

Cynthia and Sandi, also psych colleagues, sat with me as I underwent drip chemo and I started to fade as the medicine poisoned my body.

Ted, the administrator in our department, sent funny videos to make me laugh and memes about the Cubs to cheer me up. Sometimes he would come over on trash night to drag my cans to the curb.

Tracy, a faculty member in the History Department, showed up at our house in the middle of a snowstorm to shovel and plow our long driveway.

My friend Josh would regularly text me from Texas to check in and see how I was doing or send me a funny picture to make me laugh.

One of my students, Miranda, who had become like part of our family, babysat the girls so that Kelly and I could slip away for a bit of time alone.

We received over two hundred "thinking of you" cards filled with encouragement that covered our hallway doors, just off the kitchen, from friends and family.

Isaac would call and ask for advice about research even though he didn't need the help, just to help me feel normal and useful and laugh at my jokes when they made less sense than normal.

Michael, another colleague from the Psychology Department, had blue rubber bracelets made that had my name and "Lord hear our prayers" next to a dove symbol that was worn by friends, family, as well as strangers, throughout the campus, Wheaton, our church, and my hometown. I received a picture from Kenya of refugee pastors living in the Kakuma refugee camp wearing the bracelets with a message to let me know they were praying for me.

Even our little fifteen-pound Terrier-Shih Tzu-we think-dog Buddy seemed to sense when I was in a lot of pain and would come lay in front of me with his head on my chest when I couldn't get off the couch.

Every offer, every gift, every ride, every note was a mixed blessing. Each one communicated that I was loved and cared for by my community. And they also triggered a stubborn reflex in me that resisted receiving. During the extremely brief period when I could still drive my own car and tie my own shoes, stubborn pride won out. Then, as my illness progressed, the tug and pull between independence and depending on others gave way to accepting the help others offered. I was slowly forced to admit that when I wanted people the least is when I needed them the most.

CHAPTER 6

Where Is God in the Storm?

Making Meaning of Disasters

O NE VISIT to the hospital for tests, scans, and treatments blended into the next. Most days I laid in bed feeling completely depleted. During those quiet moments, when I was too uncomfortable to sleep or concentrate on work or even pleasure reading, I had plenty of time to wonder why I had been afflicted with colorectal cancer. In a seemingly endless loop, I would mentally review all that Kelly and I had learned about the disease.

The average age when people are diagnosed with colorectal cancer is seventy-two. I was thirty-five.

Close family members having the disease increased the risk of getting it, yet no one in my extended family had ever been diagnosed.

Having ulcerative colitis or Crohn's disease increased the risk. I had neither.

People who smoke cigarettes were at higher risk. I never smoked a cigarette in my lifetime.

My mind was a busy cyclone of reasoning, trying desperately to answer the question *why*.

People often have a difficult time getting our heads around what has happened because disasters can cause meaning ruptures that trigger existential questions and concerns. The crisis can disrupt our sense of purpose in life, making us more aware of our mortality or more aware of loneliness and isolation. None of these existential concerns, nor the answer to the question "why," have easy resolutions.

In my case, the lingering *why* questions constantly swirled in and out of my consciousness.

One of the theories I teach my grad students is the "just-world hypothesis." Although it may seem naïve, most of us naturally believe that if we are good, good things will happen. We don't announce it at dinner parties, or wear the slogan emblazoned on T-shirts, but we naturally move through the world operating from this deep underlying assumption. So it's natural that we struggle to make sense of the unpredictability of bad things happening to good people, because it forces us to admit that there is much over which we have no control. Disasters turn what we thought we knew about the world and about God upside down. In the wake of disaster, we try to make meaning by asking "Why?" And our instinctive response is to make sense of the incongruity by creating "reasons" for what we, and others, have endured.

Why me?

Why is this happening when I have this young family to love and support?

Why don't I get to grow old with Kelly?

Why might my daughters grow up without a father?

Why is this happening when I've been given such a clear sense of vision and calling for work in disaster ministry?

These sorts of questions kept bubbling up for me. But no matter how many times I asked them, I struggled to find a satisfactory answer for why.

I knew I wasn't alone in asking many of these questions. Others who, like me, are diagnosed with stubborn or rehabilitating diseases ask them. Parents who suffer the loss of a child ask them. Survivors of catastrophic natural disasters will question why their home is the only one destroyed in a neighborhood while another homeowner whose house is the only one left standing will also ask similar questions.

While I'd witnessed enough misery professionally to know that sometimes bad things just happen, that head knowledge didn't keep me from pressing for a logical rationale for my diagnosis.

One late night, lying in bed not able to sleep, I made the risky decision to watch a movie starring Joseph Gordon-Levitt called *50/50*. The morose premise of the movie is that a young man in his late twenties is diagnosed with cancer and given a fifty-fifty chance of survival. My curiosity overrode the internal warning signals alerting me that choosing to view a movie with a fifty-fifty chance of a young man dying from cancer was *not* a wise choice.

After all the relevant diagnostics have been performed, the young man sits across a stately wooden desk from a somber doctor in a white lab coat. When the doctor tells him that he has a rare form of cancer in his spine, the protagonist is unable to make sense of what he's learning. Though he's heard the words, and at some level understands what they mean, their reality is virtually incomprehensible.

"A tumor?" he asks, with a look of surprise on his face that almost belies amusement. "Me?"

Dumbfounded, the young man protests as I had, "That doesn't make any sense, though. I don't smoke. I don't drink." And to underscore his goodness, he goes one step further than I had by emphatically adding, "I *recycle*."

For the first time in a long time, I felt less alone. Obviously, bad things shouldn't befall those who are good enough to *recycle*.

What the audience recognizes as absurd—and in my best moments I also recognized as ludicrous—made complete sense to me! The natural reaction to a disaster is to attempt to make meaning of what has happened to us. Our first instinct is to assume that there is a logical cause for our suffering. And we wrestle—with ourselves and with God—to make meaning of our situations by identifying and naming that cause.

But sometimes we just can't.

Other times we blame ourselves.

Was it bad dietary choices?

Was it my lack of exercise?

Was it caused by a lack of sleep?

Many people who experience misfortune believe that God is punishing them. The man who was promiscuous as a teenager believes that his infertility as an adult is divine retribution for his actions as a youth. And in spite of reassurance from doctors that she is not culpable, a mother who gives birth to a child with a life-threatening illness suspects that she is in some way responsible. I regularly encountered these sorts of struggles from my clients when I was working as a therapist. But these sort of questions are not limited to the confines of the counseling office. Our research has found that these kinds of questions are common when tragedy strikes.

Though I didn't believe that God was punishing me, I continued to search for reasons I was suffering. I racked my brain for what might have caused my cancer.

Eventually, in the mental litany of searching for answers, I'd review the early years of my life.

Was it because I grew up drinking well water contaminated by pesticides? I'd read online that a study out of Australia had proven that drinking tainted water increased the risk of colon cancer.

Was it because of the yellow acne medication I'd taken as a teenager? I looked into the medication after my diagnosis and found out it had been yanked from the market because of lawsuits from users who prematurely developed colon cancer in their thirties. Was I seriously facing life-threatening cancer because I'd had zits in high school?

Was it a combination of some or all of these different factors?

Sometimes we blame others.

As part of my desperate search for meaning, I thought I might have a legal case against the company that made

the acne medicine. I reached out to my parents, old doctors, and a pharmacy but no one had medical records from
that long ago still available to help me prove I had taken it.
Then I thought about the possibility of suing the specialist
whose neglect had allowed the tumor inside of me to grow
for another full year. I wanted an answer for the cause
of my cancer that would stand up in court. Even if such a
victory didn't heal me, I thought it would offer some sort
of meaning. I wanted answers and I wanted restitution. I
wanted to point to something tangible, something or someone other than me, for what was happening.

And yet, while a legal victory would have offered some
satisfaction, I knew that it would not ultimately satisfy my
"why" questions. I first met J. Steven Picou after Hurricane
Katrina. He was a professor of sociology at the University
of South Alabama at the time and had conducted research
on those who pursued adversarial litigation against Exxon
after the *Exxon Valdez* oil spill. But Picou discovered that
those in the local community who sued actually suffered
more psychological distress than those who didn't because
of the long contentious upward battle they faced. In some
cases, restitution needs to be made, as was the case following the oil spill, but it doesn't guarantee closure or healing.

As for myself, at this point in my cancer battle I knew
that I didn't have the energy to be able to battle cancer
while taking on a long, drawn-out legal battle. After finishing my cancer treatments, though, the "why" questions
resurfaced, and so I decided to consult with a lawyer. But I

learned that the specialist who had misdiagnosed me had a generic medical note with boilerplate recommendations, including recommending a colonoscopy. Even though he told me something different verbally, and these recommendations weren't included in my checkout materials, I had no case.

Like with the tech who had told me "God only tests the strong," I was reminded of the importance of forgiveness.

In the aftermath of Superstorm Sandy, a colleague of mine deployed to help those whose lives had been upended when Sandy made landfall. She met a man whose roof had been blown away by gale-force winds. Like a Lego home under construction, the walls remained, but the house was roofless. When she approached the survivor, she expected him to be in a lot of distress. Instead he quipped, "Sometimes you have to lose the roof to see the stars." A realist may read this and think this is yet another example of blind optimism or just another pat answer to a difficult situation. But the way my colleague described his response, the survivor seemed authentic in how he had come to understand what he'd been through. And even when there is no silver lining or answers to be found, the search itself has value and purpose.

Wanting to understand if my diagnosis meant my girls might someday be more at risk, I visited a geneticist for a consultation. After studying all the data available to him, he could only surmise, "On paper you look like that small random group where there's a mutation."

That, of course, is the professional way of saying, "We can't identify a satisfying reason you have cancer. You just *do*."

A few days after I'd watched *50/50*, I was at the treatment center, getting ready for radiation, positioning myself on the table that would slide into the CT machine. Covered in just a dingy hospital gown, I felt vulnerable. Unprotected. Alone. In this state of self-pity, I continued to lament that no one I knew, who was *not* a fictional movie character, could relate to my experience.

The medical technician who'd helped me up onto the table operated a switch so that the tray on which I was laying would slowly shuttle me into position inside the machine. Within a treatment room, the machine itself was the size of a small truck. At the center is what looks like a sterile, well-lit, white cave. As the tray on which I was lying was slowly slid into the cave, a compelling image gripped me.

With the eyes of my heart, I saw someone else being carefully placed inside a cave. It was Jesus' body being carried into another tomb. Into the dark, dank hole his followers carefully placed his body in a cave that had been carved out of a hillside. That dehydrated body that had been flogged and beaten, that was bruised and cut, even plunged with a sword, had been wrapped in cloths—as it had been at his birth—and laid carefully inside the tomb. Then Jesus' helpers rolled a large stone in front of the opening to the tomb, to prevent anyone from disturbing the body.

During the entire treatment, I savored the nearness of this one who knew what my life was like because he had endured suffering. In a fresh way I understood, in my deep places, that Christ had gone before me and could relate to my pain. In a very palpable and visceral sense, I was no longer alone. And I was keenly aware that the peace I felt was not contingent on the outcome of my battle. Whether I lived or I died, I was loved. And that was something cancer could not take from me.

That single insight was life-altering. When I allowed myself to entertain thoughts of losing my battle with cancer, I felt extremely anxious and undone. I worried about my girls. I worried about my wife. I grieved that the gift of doing work I loved was being cut short. But when Christ joined me in the tomb, in that particular moment as I slowly emerged out of the machine, those natural worries were superseded by a higher order of meaning. A powerful sense of peace washed over me as I soaked in the reality that, even if I could not escape its grip, Jesus had already conquered death on my behalf. No matter what I would face, Christ had gone ahead to clear a way for my healing, whether in this life or the next.

Although research was the last thing on my mind at the time, my experience of finding meaning in the tomb resonated with findings my colleagues and I discovered. Some of our research has shown that people who are able to find spiritual meaning amid their disaster experience have lower rates of posttraumatic stress disorder symptoms. This type of meaning is not easily or immediately found, and in the initial throes of catastrophe it often escapes us. But we learned that striving to make meaning out of suffering can yield positive benefits similar to actually finding answers—at least for a period of time. Over the long haul, studies suggest it's better for our well-being to make meaning of our tragedies than to remain in a permanent state of quest. Though I'd not been consciously "seeking" meaning in that moment, it had graciously washed over me in a powerful and transforming way.

That is, meaning that helps us survive and recover from tragedy is much more likely to be found in the *when*, *what*, and *how* we engage with our struggle than in the *why* questions we tend to ask.

When the scan was complete, I was extracted from the machine—first feet, then torso, then finally my head. As I was shuttled back out into the land of the living, I pictured Jesus rising from the tomb, shaking off his burial cloths, and stepping out of the tomb. The work he'd done while he was in there, conquering the powers of sin and death, had been accomplished on my behalf. And because he had been victorious, I would be as well.

Graciously, the freedom I experienced wasn't contingent on the outcome of my disease. If I lived, Christ understood my sufferings and won my victory. I would live with him. If I died, Christ understood my sufferings and won my victory. I would live with him. After countless attempts to find answers, I realized no single answer was going to make everything okay.

I was reminded that God never promised to answer

all our why questions—but God has promised to give us himself.

The comfort I eventually found did not come in the form of "right" answers, but in God himself. He promises to be with us even in the most terrifying of places and times (Ps. 46:1). We can't mistake his goodness, which he promises us in this life (Ps. 27:13), for the absence of hard things. When I emerged from my sterile medical tomb, I was at peace. Finding God had come more to me than finding answers.

CHAPTER 7

FEMA X Codes

Grappling with Ambiguous Loss

SOON AFTER my diagnosis I knew I'd need surgery to remove the tumor in my colon and growth from my pelvis. During one of my weekly regular appointments with Dr. Patel, he asked, "And did you decide where you want the colostomy bag?"

"Excuse me?" I queried.

I felt my heart racing.

"What are you talking about?" I asked, glancing desperately between Kelly and Dr. Patel. "This is the first I'm hearing of this."

A colostomy is a surgery that diverts the end of the colon, or large intestine, rerouting it through an opening in the abdominal wall. This stoma is where the person's waste is expelled from the body. However, unlike the regular route, the stoma doesn't have a valve to control flow. A colostomy can be a temporary measure during the healing process from the cancer surgery. But because of where my tumor was located, the surgery would mean a permanent change in the way the body functions, including relying on a colostomy bag, or "pouch." The possibility terrified me.

Even though I was fatigued and sometimes disoriented, I knew that if the possibility of permanently losing bowel function had *ever* been mentioned, it would have been a conversation Kelly and I would have had together at some point already.

Dr. Patel continued casually, as if the world I'd always known had not just come crashing down around me.

"Your tests," he explained, "show the tumor is low enough that you'll probably need—"

His mouth kept moving, and sounds kept coming out of him, but I could no longer follow them. I was in shock, unable to process what was happening.

"Kelly," I interrupted Dr. Patel, "is this something that was discussed and I forgot?"

Having been more of an absent-minded professor lately than I usually was, I was aware that I'd definitely dropped a few mental balls lately.

"No," she answered slowly. "It's not a conversation we've had with anyone."

Because I did trust Dr. Patel, the only explanations I could come up with was that the doctors and nurses for whom these procedures were routine assumed that I knew that excising a cancerous tumor from the colon often necessitated a colostomy. Or, maybe this had fallen through the cracks because I had so many people taking care of me everyone assumed someone else had shared the news.

Noticing I had freaked out, Dr. Patel calmly explained,

"A colostomy gives you the best chance of living. The recommendation has been that we take as much of the organ as we can."

"Surely there has to be something else that can be done or some way this doesn't have to be permanent?"

Glancing at my face, Dr. Patel could read my hesitance.

"Why would you want to leave any chance?" he asked.

I thought the answer to that was obvious: *Because I don't want a colostomy.*

"Wait. There's got to be another way," I begged.

"Jamie, you want to keep the big picture in mind. Which is worse? Having a colostomy or not being alive?"

What could I say?

I wanted to live.

In the days that followed, I continued the conversation but this time with God, asking him to make a different way forward possible, praying that I could avoid a colostomy. After meeting with my other doctors for their advice, I sought out three more opinions from surgeons not affiliated with the cancer center. They all recommended the colostomy. Because I had received such great care from the cancer center, I decided to stay put and chose Dr. Campbells as my surgeon. The two most common comments I heard from health-care staff about her were, "She likes everything done in a particular way," and "She fights for her patients." Although she was clearly a no-nonsense sort of person, she was incredibly compassionate and empathetic to my concerns.

The morning of surgery, Kelly and I arrived to check in at 6 a.m. sharp. We were directed to sit in the waiting room until my name was called. Then we were led back to a private pre-op room with a tall skinny window that looked into the hallway. I could see others being hoisted away on beds as they passed by on the way to surgery. An aid yanked a thin curtain shut in front of the window as I changed from my sweats and T-shirt into a standard hospital-issue, ugly greenish-blue patterned gown. It was freezing in my room. I slipped on the hospital-issued socks, which were made from a thick synthetic that had a thin wavy rubber tread on each side of the socks to help keep patients from slipping.

As Kelly and I waited, we were visited by a battery of helping professionals: nurses, techs, an anesthesiologist, and Dr. Campbells. I made one final plea to Dr. Campbells, anxiously reminding her how much I hoped I wouldn't need a colostomy.

Nodding, she once again assured me, "I'll do everything I can for you. But I won't know for certain until I get in there."

I was still not at all resigned to the possibility of living with a pouch outside my body that would collect my stool. Dr. Campbells had promised that if there was any way to avoid a colostomy, she would. She wouldn't know until she was doing the surgery.

"Yes," I hedged anxiously, "but it might not be necessary."

"Right . . . if it's not needed, I promise I won't do it," she said. "But it's more likely we will need to."

"Okay," I conceded.

Dr. Campbells was our last visitor before I was wheeled away and put under anesthesia. The last thing I remember was Kelly walking alongside me, holding my hand as I was being whisked off to the operating room as I fell into a deep sleep.

When I regained consciousness four hours later, my life was inalterably changed.

"Did they—did they have to do the surgery?" I groggily asked Kelly.

Before she could answer I clumsily fumbled through IV lines, tubing, and my gown in search of my stomach. My hands felt like lead weights, and between my numb fingertips and thick dressing and bandages, I couldn't tell what I was feeling.

"Yes, Dr. Campbells had to give you a colostomy," Kelly gently replied.

I was in the hospital for two weeks after surgery before coming home. About halfway through my first week recovering in the hospital, my biopsy results came back.

"We found cancer in the mass," said Dr. Campbells in a quiet voice. She continued to discuss the results. I could see her lips move, but the room fell silent, like the moment we find Harry Potter in The Prisoner of Askaban, seemingly exhaling his last breath as his spirit starts to leave his motionless body after being attacked and left for dead.

Although I did not fear I was breathing my last breath, after hearing the word cancer, it felt like my last ounce of hope was slowly leaving my body.

Instead of having the muffled silence pierced with an Expecto Patronum spell, the deafness that had befallen my hospital room was broken after hearing Dr. Campbells say, "Stage IV cancer. It's officially Stage IV cancer." And, like Harry, I found myself jolted back to reality gasping for air.

After another week in the hospital I was discharged and was able to go home.

Still in agony from the surgery, I was not safe to stand on my own and couldn't walk without assistance. To stand was excruciating, especially the pain in my abdomen. An incision had been cut that started two inches below my belly button and stopped just four inches shy of my chest. Any slight touch to my chest felt like absorbing the fabled Bruce Lee one-inch punch that sent opponents flying across the room. To make matters worse, I couldn't *sit* either. Dr. Campbells had removed a significant portion of my colon when cutting out the cancer tumor. She also removed over twenty lymph nodes from my pelvis region when taking out the mass. My body had undergone the equivalent of four major surgeries during one operation.

Since I wasn't capable of walking up the stairs to our bedroom, Kelly had set up the downstairs guest room just off our kitchen for me to recover. I remained nearly bed-ridden on our white daybed for close to a month. Most of my time was spent laying on my side. On rare occasions I briefly laid on my back, slightly reclined. The only times I got up were to go to the restroom or when the home health nurse visited. Every step I took felt like my body was being split in two. The pain was so great at times it was hard to identify where it was located. Pain had swallowed me whole, like the big fish that had swallowed up Jonah in the Old Testament. I took strong medications to try and dull the pain, but I hated them because of how cloudy they made my thinking. I could barely think already because of the pain, and the meds just made it worse.

I was a stranger in my own body.

I had never experienced anything like this. "Pain" didn't do justice to what I was experiencing. I wasn't just hurting physically and emotionally; my soul ached.

This is what death feels like, I thought to myself, like the person who can't explain a sudden sense of doom right before having a heart attack.

I first read Philip Yancey's *Where's God When It Hurts?* in college after Mark Gallagher had recommended it to me. More recently I had assigned it and discussed it with each new cohort of graduate students in the crisis counseling course I taught. I read it again when I first started my cancer treatments. Reflecting on what I had gleaned from Yancey's work, I realized I wasn't just in pain. I was *suffering*.

About four days after arriving home, I finally saw myself in a mirror without a shirt on for the first time. Although Kelly had been caring for my wound in bed, this was the first time I would lay eyes on the full extent of the changes in my body. I saw it all. There was a small gashlike scar where a port had been inserted in my chest. Railroadlike scars ran up and down my abdomen.

My eye was drawn to my colostomy pouch just above my waist.

I hated it, and all it represented.

It jumped out at me like the brightly spray-painted Xs tattooed on homes around New Orleans that Hurricane Katrina had devastated. A large majority of the city's buildings had been painted with what FEMA calls "X codes." Beside the main entrance to a home or commercial building, teams of rescuers painted what looked like a huge X, most commonly in bright orange spray paint. In each quadrant of the symbol—bottom, left, top, and right—rescuers would report that they'd surveyed the structure and note what they'd discovered inside. It was an efficient way to communicate to other teams of rescuers which structures had been checked.

When a search team entered the building, they'd mark a single diagonal slash near the main entrance, indicating that a search was in progress. When they exited the building, they would complete the communication by crossing the line with another, forming a large X. The space at the bottom of the X listed the number of people who'd been found inside. When two numbers were listed, the first indicated the number of survivors and the second indicated the number of corpses found. The quadrant on the left indicated which rescue crew had searched the building. Custom initials would identify the team that had performed the search operation. The top quadrant showed the date that rescuers had searched. Finally, the right quadrant indicated other critical information about the search, such as "RATS," for rodents, or "NE," for "No entry." Studying these X codes while wandering through New Orleans' Ninth Ward was like walking through a cemetery. While no identifying details were offered, FEMA's X codes were at times a testimony to life, and also a marker of death. As I gazed in the bathroom mirror, fixated on my X, my colostomy, I felt unalterably marked by death.

As a result of the marvel of modern communication, the world was watching helplessly as planes flew into New York's Twin Towers, as Hurricane Katrina made landfall on the Gulf Coast, as Haiti was shaken by an earthquake, and as Japan was pummeled by a tsunami. And from the comfort of our Pottery Barn couches, we glimpsed only a small portion of what victims and survivors endured. Yes, we were horrified. Yes, we grieved. We may have even texted a donation to the Red Cross. But as we necessarily returned to the rhythms of our lives, what we most wanted to believe was that survivors would hunker down during impact and then continue on with their lives as if the disaster never happened. While that wish may never have even surfaced to consciousness, we wanted to believe that survivors would receive the help they needed to return to their "normal" lives as quickly as we did.

That's exactly what I'd wanted to believe about my illness. Despite the dismal survival odds, I wanted to believe that if I could make it through the grueling treatments and surgery, I could begin to heal and return to life as I'd once known it. I might have a physical scar or two to remind me of what I'd endured, but I desperately wanted to believe that life would continue as it had been before my body was invaded by cancer. Kelly and I would continue parenting our precious girls through adolescence and into adulthood. I'd continue building and growing programs at the Humanitarian Disaster Institute. In years to come, through eyes of gratitude and faith, we'd look back on our "cancer season" and give thanks that it was behind us.

The X on my body, the pouch that hung from just above my waist, refuted the narrative that life would return to the way it had been. While I was technically surviving, I hadn't made it through my disaster unscathed. The ugly X screamed that I would never be the same. It was a constant reminder of my cancer and that I might not make it. I was like the flooded Ninth Ward homes in New Orleans—still standing but hallowed out—not by water but from pain and suffering. I felt like I had been marked for death.

Several months before the tragedy America experienced on 9/11, I remember running through O'Hare International Airport, zipping past a security guard who cheered me on—just shy of giving me a high five—as I ran for my gate. The first time Kelly and I flew out of O'Hare after the bombing of the Twin Towers, additional security checkpoints had been established. Security guards eyed everyone as a potential suspect. Members of the military were armed, and they used weapon-sniffing dogs. No one in uniform was high-fiving. Life after disaster is different.

Trauma researchers refer to this phenomenon as "ambiguous loss." Even though life might start to look as it once did, outwardly, something significant about one's way of life is lost. Following the tragic loss of life after 9/11, the nation's sense of security was lost. After Katrina, a part of New Orleans' culture was lost. These sorts of losses are hard to identify, making it even more challenging to find closure. The result is that people's ability to grieve is delayed and complicated.

And just as the new skyline of New York City, sans Twin Towers, has been a constant reminder of devastation, my colostomy was that kind of reminder for me. I'd been at war, and I'd been wounded. Every time I looked in the mirror or glanced down at my stomach, I was reminded that cancer had landed a devastating blow to my body. Because I was so weak and fragile, I felt like cancer had already won.

The X on my body, the lasting mark of loss and a reminder of death, rippled throughout the rest of my life. There was no going back to life as I had known it—and I wondered just how much more life I had ahead.

CHAPTER 8

Katrina Mardi Gras Trailers

Establishing New Rhythms

THANKSGIVING WAS just around the corner, and everyone in the Chicagoland area was gearing up for winter. For the first time since my surgery, I had good moments where the *spring* of my recovery process seemed to be on the horizon. Like almost any given spring in the Chicago area, it started with an occasional good day here and there, like having the strength to stand at the kitchen table with my family while they ate dinner. I still couldn't sit more than a couple minutes at a time but was glad to be able to just be with them. And just as quickly as the good days appeared, my progress would stall or revert.

Over the previous six months I had undergone tests, completed oral chemo, finished radiation, had a four-in-one cancer surgery, and was now living with a colostomy. Thankfully I was on the other side of the treatments, but it was still too early to tell if they'd been successful in eradicating the cancer from my body. Regardless of how effective the treatments might have been, I knew that recovering from what I had been through was going to take time.

Still, I was grateful to still be alive.

After dropping the girls at school and preschool, Kelly and I headed toward the cancer center to see Dr. Patel. After reviewing my charts and labs, Dr. Patel told me that an interdisciplinary panel of experts from the cancer center had discussed my case. He wanted me to start a six-month round of drip chemo treatments as soon as possible.

The news was devastating. It felt like hearing, "It's cancer" all over again. Hearing I needed six more months of chemo forced me, once again, to face the seriousness of my diagnosis. It moved cancer back to the forefront of my life, just as I thought I was about to finally leave cancer behind.

My body was weakened by all the treatments I had gone through. Over the past summer I had reasoned with myself that I could survive three months of chemo and radiation. After all, it's just a summer. But six months of chemo, now, after everything I've gone through? I felt like my legs had been knocked out from under me. I just didn't know if I could do it. I understood the importance of zapping any possible rogue cancer cells, but the thought of subjecting myself to more treatments felt unbearable.

Dr. Patel recommended that I start chemo the week before Thanksgiving. He explained that I'd have to come to the cancer center to be hooked up to the drip for four hours at a time and then go home with a chemo pack that would continue to pump chemo through my port into my body for an additional thirty-six hours, at which point I would go back and get disconnected. I'd alternate one week on and one week off. We discussed the pros and cons of the additional treatment as I prepared for chemo. But Dr. Patel was very clear that not receiving the chemo treatments was likely a death sentence. I would have negated all that I had endured already. Overwhelmed, unable to process what all of his recommendations meant, I assured Dr. Patel that I'd weigh my options carefully—but only after pushing back against every reason given by asking *why*. I even asked to have someone from his staff send me some clinical trial research outcomes; I wanted to see hard evidence before making my decision.

In the car on the way home, Kelly and I discussed whether I should undertake another round of chemo. We also weighed the option of at least postponing chemo for two weeks so that we could visit our families in southern Illinois and Indiana over Thanksgiving before launching into the grueling regimen.

As we were discussing it, my cell phone lit up with a call from Dr. Patel.

"Hello?" I answered, knowing he couldn't be calling with news any less disturbing than what I'd just received.

"Jamie," he began, "I want to make sure you understand what's at stake."

"Okay," I agreed, waiting for him to continue. I felt like we'd just had this conversation—but he seemed to want to underscore his advice.

"Postponing chemo will substantially lower your odds of survival," he said in a serious tone. He'd been clear that refusing chemo was a possible death sentence, but he wanted to make sure I also understood the risks of waiting too long to begin.

He continued, "Every week you postpone treatment, your survival odds decrease."

I considered his words.

Then, after a long pause, he added, "At the same time, social support has been associated with more positive outcomes among cancer patients. If there's anyone you want to see, anything you want to do, this might be that time. But keep in mind the risks of waiting too long or choosing not to do another round of chemo. You really need this."

"I understand," I said. "Thank you for calling."

I was familiar with the kind of data with which Dr. Patel was working. I also knew how important emotional health and well-being were to survival odds.

As had been the case when I awoke with a colostomy bag, both Kelly and I were starting to understand that life would never be the same. What I hadn't anticipated was how long we would have to figure out how to live life in limbo. After surgery we didn't know how long we'd be bullied by medical mayhem, but we did agree that we needed to find a way to move forward that was life-giving for our whole family. Ultimately, Kelly and I agreed that I'd begin treatments the Monday after the holiday.

We left to visit our families two days before Thanksgiving. I was really concerned if I could physically undertake such a long drive. Going on a road trip with Kelly and the girls felt like an adventure, since the only time I had left the house since my surgery was for doctors' appointment or treatments. Though I still wasn't comfortable sitting for more than a couple minutes at a time, I endured the five-hour drive. I stayed on top of my pain medicine, sat on several pillows, and alternated leaning awkwardly on each hip, but I did it, which I claimed as a small victory. It felt wonderfully normal to be with our families for Thanksgiving meals, to eat familiar food, to play familiar board games, and to see my girls' faces light up as they interacted with relatives. Kelly, the girls, and I snuggled up on the sofa in her parents' living room and took a family picture like we had done so many times during the holidays. My parents also volunteered to watch our girls so that we could go to the movie theater in Robinson, the town next to Oblong that had opened since I'd lived there.

Before the movie we visited our friends Dave and Janette, whom I had known growing up. The first time Kelly came home with me was to their wedding, which I was in. We laughed as we recalled Kelly and I swing dancing at their reception and wrapping their car in toilet paper at their hotel. We also talked about our wedding, where Dave was my groomsman. We picked right up as though no time had lapsed.

After buying our tickets for the newest Hunger Games movie, *Catching Fire*, we warmed up in the lobby. Standing in line for the Sprite and popcorn we'd share, I was grateful that—excluding the pain I felt with every step I took and the inflatable yellow donut pillow I'd smuggled in—we felt like a normal couple again. The sweet fragrance of warm buttered popcorn wafted throughout the theater. What could be more normal than that?

One of the central plotlines in *Catching Fire* is that heroine Katnis is trying to save Peeta's life. While others in the theater were enraptured by the story, the drama that paralleled our lives was hitting a little too close to home. Feeling the weighty emotional sting in our bodies, exchanging only a few words, Kelly and I both agreed to leave the theater.

Though too early to go to bed, and too rural to host hip nighttime coffee shops, I remembered that a new twenty-four-hour Super Walmart had also opened in Robinson. (Almost as exciting as the movie theater!) Kelly and I drove to it, if only to work off some of the anxiety that had forced its way into our date night. In the condiment aisle Kelly remembered we needed salad dressing at home, and we both cracked up when she picked up the largest bottle of buttermilk ranch dressing either one of us had ever seen. Realizing we'd systematically covered the first five aisles, we decided to zigzag our way through every aisle in the store.

Though for many this would qualify as the worst date night ever, it is a precious memory for me. We felt like *us* again. Our purposeful walking was more like the spiritual act of walking a labyrinth than simply accruing steps in a big-box store. Before we left, we perused a monthly wall calendar of Chuck Norris memes, with classics like, "Chuck Norris once ran on a treadmill—it couldn't keep up." It felt so good, and so right, to laugh together again. Although we didn't finish *Catching Fire* that night, or even purchase the world's largest bottle of buttermilk ranch dressing, we rediscovered the sacred in the mundane.

When I was first diagnosed, I felt like my life was over. Cancer threatened to change everything my family cherished. And to be fair, it had swept through our lives like a hurricane, damaging health, security, time together, and our peace of mind. But I'd also begun to notice that some of the most solid places in the storm we were weathering were many of the familiar rhythms and traditions we'd continued to practice. During the storm, these knit us together and strengthened us as a family.

Thanksgiving had also served as an anchor for our family. We were surrounded by people who loved us fiercely and who were fighting alongside us. Even the mundane of Walmart had offered us holy refuge. Embracing these experiences had been like finding dry ground as the storm waters began to rise once again.

As Kelly and I drove back toward my parents' home, past shells of barren winter cornstalks, I was reminded of an exhortation to University of Southern Mississippi faculty from the school's president when the school reopened after Katrina. He encouraged us to provide normalcy for students, offering, "Whatever you were doing before Katrina, go back to doing that now." In the years that followed, I continued to employ this approach to help disaster survivors I encountered or studied around the globe.

On my multiple trips to Japan after the 3/11 disaster, I sipped tea with survivors who were living in temporary houses that looked like tiny sheds. As we chatted I heard the soothing sounds of the ocean—which many still cherished but also feared—lapping in the distance. They'd drunk tea before so much of their lives was washed away, and they drank tea after. The ritual of having tea brought them together when they needed each other's support the most.

In Haiti I worshiped with a congregation as they clapped hands of praise in a makeshift tent church that had been erected next to a rubble memorial. The rubble was all that was left of the church building that had collapsed during the quake, killing many who had been worshiping inside. They worshiped before the quake, and they worshiped after it. Through the ritual of worship, they joined with one another and with God in the face of calamity.

After a long day helping along the Mississippi Gulf Coast following Katrina, I was invited to a potluck dinner with survivors who'd gone from living in a neighborhood of stately colonial homes, passed from one generation to the next, to their new neighborhood: a fleet of FEMA trailers. I was surprised when I found some had decked out their FEMA trailers for Mardi Gras in bright purple and gold colors. Some had glowing green and purple lights lining the horizontal cylinders they now called home. Giant sparkle-covered masks and other decorations were plastered on bland exterior walls. In true southern fashion, some had even built out small front porches off the front of their FEMA trailers. They'd celebrated before Katrina, and they were celebrating after Katrina.

Disaster survivors taught me it was possible, even if for only brief moments, to continue living life in the wake of catastrophe. During my extended cancer disaster, my family doing what we'd been doing prior to my diagnosis was critical to stabilizing our lives during the storm and in its aftermath.

Remembering the advice of the University of Southern Mississippi's president, I began to notice the other natural rhythms of our lives that were keeping us afloat. One of those for us was church attendance. Although a lot of weeks I couldn't get out of bed, there were weeks when I could. Most of the time my mind was so cloudy from the chemo that I couldn't retain or follow what was being preached about or discussed in Sunday school. However, at times, though they were brief, I felt like myself. One Sunday morning I was actually tracking the discussion and offered some comment about existential philosophers. In my mind I was like, *Wow, thank God, that stuff is still in me somewhere.* I had a sense of joy and hope that normal might be possible again. While still reflecting on the class discussion, I then stepped out of class and into the restroom, only to be surprised that there weren't any urinals. I had accidentally walked right into the women's restroom. Though no one else was in the restroom or noticed my mistake, I was embarrassed. Still, I could find hope in that experience of being able to think clearly enough to contribute something intellectually. I was also learning to laugh and find humor when things like this happened.

When I was in private practice, our office had a small

wooden sign in the waiting room that read, "Normal is a setting on a washing machine." And while there's no true normal when it comes to navigating a personal storm, plenty of other rhythms helped to stabilize our family during it. Mundane tasks as simple as helping the girls with homework or pitching in to wash the dishes—even when it required all the strength I had—helped life to feel normal.

When I encourage survivors of disaster to return to what they were doing prior to impact, I don't mean that everything will return to the way it was. It won't. But I'm convinced that people do benefit from carving out calm in the chaos. It buffers the roller-coaster effect inherent in so many disasters. For some, that will mean opting for rhythms in which they'll see familiar faces—at church, a child's school, or a neighborhood potluck. For others, maintaining a bit of the schedule they'd once held can be grounding. For some, that means rising early for a walk or meditation. For others, it can mean meeting a jogging buddy for coffee instead of a run. Others will carve out a short period of time each day for work or hobbies that are life-giving. And like our family traveling to be with extended family for Thanksgiving, choosing to be in places that feed the soul can also offer comfort and stability. There can be healing and stability in returning to normal rhythms and routines.

During that season, we purposed to adopt the mindset of a friend of Kelly's. When she helped to care for a friend with cancer, this woman noticed how similar it was to other life seasons. She remarked, "When you go to college, you 'do' school. When your kids are little, you 'do' childrearing. Now it's time to 'do' cancer." I found her perspective helpful, as a reminder that you still have to "do," even in the midst of difficulty.

That "doing" took on a whole new meaning for me during this time period. As the type of person who loves creating to-do lists and crossing off tasks throughout the day, the tasks that weren't accomplished—even the ones I held in my head that never made it to the list—became laden with meaning. For instance, if doing the dishes was going to sap the energy I needed to snuggle with my girls when they got home from school, I could actively choose to not do the dishes. And other times doing the dishes felt like a small victory. Similarly, because my body needed what felt like an inordinate amount of rest, I begrudged the time "wasted" by napping, when I wasn't "accomplishing" anything. But when I began to see napping as an action, I learned to embrace it as an important life-giving part of my new routine.

Our family also found life by creating new rhythms and traditions. In the midst of a particularly difficult week for all of us, a few weeks after my treatments had begun, Kelly suggested that we go around the dinner table and answer the question, "What was the best part of your day?" Kelly began, mentioning, "I had a good day at work." Then, moving clockwise around the table, we all shared. Chloe: "I had fun at art class. We tried painting fruit." Carlee chimed in next after a long pause, "I had fun on the playground." Colleen piped up, "Today was library day. I got to check out some new books."

"Dad, how about you?" Colleen asked. At first I was speechless. I struggled to find something positive to share. It had been a rough day—for too many days. I would have loved to have offered a "best" as robust as having worked on a research paper, or having a low-pain day, or better yet, having the energy to snuggle with her and her sisters after school.

But it finally hit me. "Right now. The best part of my day is right now, hearing about each of your days, being able to spend time at dinner with my family."

By doing the things we'd always done, and by establishing a few new family rhythms, we experienced stability in the storm.

Allowing the Waves to Wash Over You

Dealing with Pain

O NE OF THE key therapeutic methods in which I was trained is called "second-wave cognitive behavioral therapy." This approach to mental health suggests that many of the negative symptoms we experience come from faulty thinking. The client's goal, then, is to identify the negative patterns and replace them with more positive thinking patterns.

This is one method used to help clients who've endured trauma. A client who has experienced trauma because of assault, war, natural disaster, or some other catastrophic event is encouraged to notice and "catch" the troubling thought. Whenever they notice the invasive thought, they are to replace the thought with a picture of a stop sign. Professionals employing this method would coach clients, "When you feel distressed and notice the thought that's attached to that feeling, focus on that stop sign."

The goal is to interrupt the feeling loop that the thought sets in motion by choosing to focus on a different thought.

Second-wave cognitive behavioral therapy is one popular way to help those who bear the enduring effects of trauma change their experience.

For me the approach was more than theory. As the eternal optimist, pushing away negative emotions came naturally to me. When negative emotions threatened, I found a way to put a positive spin on what I was facing. When I'd first moved to Mississippi with my wife and daughter, I'd gone to study health disparities in the Delta region. I'd never intended to study disasters. As I cleared debris near our home after the storm, I worried about the security of my job and our family, thinking, *I was just in the wrong place at the wrong time.* But because this event changed the trajectory of my life and career, whenever I enter a disaster zone today I remember Mississippi and think, with gratitude, *I was in the wrong place at exactly the right time.* This ability to find good even in difficult times had always served me well.

But in numerous instances, the positive slant I assigned to the worst circumstances amid my cancer experience sometimes did more harm than good. The reassuring line I parroted to my parents after diagnosis—that I was just glad that doctors had caught my cancer in time—was a classic example of trying to replace the negative thought with a positive one. Eventually, though, idealism about what one is facing—when it doesn't jibe with reality—will give way to weariness, trauma, grief, and suffering.

During my early recovery, when I experienced pangs of

sorrow, I would practice a common cognitive behavioral therapy technique, picturing a stop sign to interrupt the disturbing thought. But the method wasn't always as successful as I would have hoped. When I'd feel overwhelmed with sorrow in a doctor's waiting room, or when I felt too much despair to appreciate one of Colleen's clever quips, the stop sign wasn't helping me. Those emotional reactions, which were pretty new for me, made me think I might be experiencing a major depressive episode. Being the psychologist that I am, I administered myself the Beck Depression Inventory, but the results didn't reveal that I met the criteria for depression. A couple of months after surgery I was well enough to meet with a psychologist. I shared my concerns with her.

"Jamie," she reflected, "it doesn't quite sound like depression to me. That's not what I'm hearing. It sounds like you're experiencing *lament*."

A sufferer laments when he or she experiences and expresses the sorrow he is feeling. When words fail, lament helps those who've endured suffering express their pain, sorrow, and grief. Lament is grief anchored in hope. The spiritual practice can also help survivors connect with their current losses. Rather than resisting negative feelings and thoughts, lament allows them. And, either communally or individually, lament makes room for a group or a person to grieve what ought rightly to be grieved. In response to a country's history of genocide or war or slavery or oppression, communities wail and lament together to express their sorrow. When responses to suffering, like despair or rage or anguish, naturally bubble to the surface, choosing lament is deciding to honestly experience one's suffering.

After the appointment with my therapist, I began to wonder what lament might look like in my life.

The South Mississippi community we lived in when Katrina struck was called Oak Grove, aptly named for its many towering oak trees. As I drove into our community for the first time after our evacuation, I felt disoriented by how the storms' gale-force winds had obliterated many of the large oaks in the heavily wooded lot I had passed on my way to our home. The oaks had withstood many storms, but not this one. There were now more uprooted oaks than rooted oaks. Many pine trees had also been torn out in this lot, which in some cases had been thrust through neighbors' homes like torpedoes. Still, to my surprise, standing pine trees now outnumbered the oaks in this expansive lot. The pine trees that survived were well-rooted yet flexible; many now leaned slanted above the ground. But they survived by being able to bend with the winds.

I realized that if I were going to have a shot at surviving cancer, I needed to take a lesson from the well-rooted pine trees I had passed. If I always tried to fight, by standing rigidly against the winds, I'd surely be uprooted like the overturned oaks.

When I'd recovered enough from surgery for Kelly to return to work part-time, physical exhaustion continued and my personal resources were diminishing. One evening Kelly was out assisting a laboring woman with her delivery and I was putting the girls down for bed. Because I wasn't yet allowed to lift more than ten pounds, that meant I hobbled into their bedrooms and coached them through their bedtime routine. That limitation was the hardest for four-year-old Carlee, who sometimes remembered that Daddy couldn't lift her and at other times needed to be reminded. It was hard on me, too.

After reading a few stories together and resisting pleas for more, I headed toward the bathroom to finish my own bedtime routine. My energy was waning, and I knew that I didn't dare lie down before making a stop in the bathroom or I'd never be able to get back up. Wearily squeezing toothpaste onto my toothbrush and spinning the top back on the tube, I began brushing my teeth.

I'd been mindlessly daydreaming, tallying the hours of sleep I might get if I was actually able to sleep through the night, when I experienced an intrusive traumatic thought that some would call a flashback.

I felt the same brutally painful sensation. Specifically, I was reliving the moment during the digital exam in which the doctor discovered the mass and realized how low it was. He was clearly surprised to be touching the tumor, and the pain I experienced when he did was blinding. I felt like I might pass out.

In the privacy of my bathroom, as I felt a similar stab of pain, the invasive thought that accompanied the painful physical sensation I experienced was, *It's happening to me again*. The way a loud noise or sudden flash of light might convince a soldier on home leave of being physically back on the field in the midst of battle, I felt as though I was actually experiencing the invasion again. I knew that the event that sets the flashback experience into motion—a sound, a sight, or in my case possibly a pain in my body—was called a "trigger event."

My impulse, of course, was to fight it—to do anything I could to make the physical pain and emotional terror stop.

As my girls read peacefully in their beds, I pictured the shiny red stop sign at the end of our street, framed by a clear blue sky. I took several deep breaths. Visualizing the shape, the color, the purpose, I mentally said the word, *Stop*. I still felt panicked. As much as I resisted the intrusive scene replaying on the tape in my mind, no amount of psychic resistance on my part delivered me from the agony I was experiencing.

Had the stop-sign trick helped me, I might not have been reminded of my therapist's suggestion that what I was experiencing, and could embrace, was lament. But because cognitive and behavioral resistance had not served me and had only frozen me in my pain, I chose to stop resisting, which third-wave cognitive behavioral therapy subscribes.

Accept this, Jamie, I mentally coached myself. *Experience what you're going through. Let the pain wash over you.*

Releasing all resistance, I stopped fighting and I allowed the pain of suffering to flow over me like waves on a beach. I *allowed* both the physical pain and the emotional pain of what I'd endured. What was different about choosing to accept what I was experiencing, instead of resisting it, was that the feelings passed over me and eventually washed away.

That scary moment that I would not have chosen really turned out to be a microcosm of a larger freedom. Though my temptation was to push away negative emotions, I was learning that when I pushed them away, they returned like a tetherball. Batting away the sadness and anger about my situation wasn't helping. I learned that it was important, and okay, for me to embrace the pain, sadness, and suffering when it surfaced. I learned that I had to experience each of the feelings trapped inside me before I could find myself on the other side of them.

Bending over to support my weight by placing both hands on the bathroom counter, I inhaled a deep cleansing breath. Though I was still exhausted, I noticed that the terror and even the physical pain that had stabbed me had dissipated. Slowly walking back to bed, I instinctively stepped gingerly to not aggravate the pain that still weekly was radiating through my body. Easing myself into bed, tucking in under our top sheet, I pulled my prayer shawl over my midsection. The knit blanket reminded me that the One who was with me is the One who gladly received my lament. Instead of grabbing my phone or iPad to squeeze in a few minutes of work before crashing, I paused to stay present to what I was feeling. Quietly weeping, I allowed the sorrow and heartache inside me to find expression— and after ten or fifteen minutes, I noticed that the traumatic feelings I'd been experiencing had passed. Lament had allowed me to experience them in such a way that I was open to experience whatever came next.

I knew my experience was not unique. About a year after Hurricane Katrina, our team was asked to evaluate a large denomination's response to the storm. As part of that research we learned that when members of one Mississippi congregation emerged from sheltering in place or returned from their exoduses, they discovered that the building where they'd once worshiped was gone. All that remained of their house of worship was a concrete slab. During the week, the pastor spread the word that they would still meet for worship like they did every week. On Sunday morning September 4, men, women, and children stood on the church's bare foundation to worship together. Because that bare concrete foundation was all that remained, the church still referred to that moment as "Slab Sunday." Without the accompaniment of an organ or a single guitar, they sang songs confirming their confidence in a merciful God. The pastor also provided a time for members to name what had been lost, in their lives and in the community. Throughout the morning, the congregation's longest worship service to date, members wept with each other, leaning on one another and on God. Long after the service had ended, they talked, hugged, and prayed for one another, feeling and expressing to each other and to God all that they'd endured. Together, they lamented.

As folks in that congregation would discover, and as I discovered, the experience of lament is not a once-and-done event. There would be countless more moments of weeping and lament for members of that church, as there would be for me, too. So, as much as I would have liked to have scheduled "lament" in convenient time slots on my Google calendar, I knew that the feelings would come when they chose. And that's exactly what happened.

Once I agreed to allow my body to experience what it was carrying, I was able to have more moments of cathartic release. One afternoon I was getting a drink of water from the kitchen when I was suddenly overcome with sorrow. Although I didn't experience a conscious thought that triggered that feeling, I was able to notice the feeling. And while I knew I had the resources—or perhaps better to say *defenses*—to put up a strong fight in hopes of avoiding the feeling, I chose to allow the sobs that begged for expression. When I became willing to give it a rest, these moments of lament became an important part of my healing process. I could become overwhelmed emotionally by a benign conversation with a friend or even a television show that wasn't particularly emotionally charged. And rather than resisting difficult emotions, as I once might have, I chose to allow those feelings expression in my body.

I also made room to lament the loss of the future I'd imagined for my life. Rather than pushing away the intrusive thoughts and negative emotions, I allowed myself to entertain them, and allowed myself to feel the hurt. I lamented the awareness that Kelly and I might not go gray and hobble into old age together. If I didn't make it, some of the memories my young girls would have of me would be from stories told by others and not their actual memories.

I grieved for the potential moments I'd never experience if my cancer returned, which I knew was a very real possibility. I wouldn't walk my girls down the aisle. I wouldn't buy a teardrop camper or old hot rod truck to pull during retirement while traveling the country with Kelly. Those horrible possibilities were always with me, but resisting them—by avoiding them, or by putting some sort of twisted rosy spin on them—had not soothed my heart. When I did let myself experience my sorrow, sadness, tears, and heavy sobbing often flowed. In these moments, all that I dreaded most washed past me like leaves being swept down a river. Although decidedly counterintuitive, this is exactly what allowed me to get on the other side of the despair.

A time to push through would come later in survivorship. Now that I could name the ambiguous losses I had experienced and feared were ahead, it was time to give myself space to grieve.

Keys to a Home Destroyed

Distinguishing between Optimism and Hope

ALTHOUGH I HAD resisted beginning the punishment of drip chemotherapy all together, I'd begun receiving treatments in early December and was now about five weeks into the grueling regime. As so many cancer survivors have reported, the way to life feels like death—because it *is* like death. Chemotherapy delivers toxic chemicals throughout the body that not only attack cancer cells, they also wreak havoc on one's immune system and other organs.

I felt like I was in a boxing match with a heavyweight boxer who was pummeling me round after round. In the first round I was knocked to the mat by radiation and chemotherapy treatments. In the second round, just as I started to feel a bit better, I had surgery to remove the cancer, delivering a blow so bad I thought my fight might be over. After feeling like I was down for the count, I got back on my feet in the third round, only to be told I had to complete another twelve *more* rounds of drip chemotherapy over six additional months. I felt pinned in the corner of the ring. I struggled to muster enough strength to keep my fists up and arms close to my body as I absorbed punch after punch.

My colleague Terri Watson from the Psychology Department had invited me to share a devotional message on what I had learned from my cancer experience with my colleagues at a daylong faculty and staff retreat before the beginning of spring semester. I knew I didn't have the stamina to make it through the full day, but I was willing to give it everything I had in order to try to offer a brief devotional. I missed teaching. I missed my relationships with my colleagues. I missed contributing to my community. I'd jotted down some reflections on my iPhone about what I'd been discovering on my cancer journey so far. Though I was looking forward to being with my colleagues, I was nervous about giving the devotional, which was uncharacteristic.

Despite the fact that I was on medical leave over the course of the fall semester, I had been trying to "contribute" as much as I was able from bed on the rare occasions I was able: scrawling disjointed book chapters, checking in with students, emailing with colleagues. And although I reminded myself constantly that my value did not depend on my productivity, I'd been looking forward to this opportunity to share something with others, especially those who'd been so supportive of my family and me.

Kelly had joined me that day, driving us through slushy streets that bordered yards filled with clean white snow and friendly snowmen, to a large hall at a church adjacent to the edge of campus where faculty had gathered for social, spiritual, and intellectual refreshment a few days before students were scheduled to return to campus. Kelly and I had timed our arrival to avoid the potentially exhausting coffee hour and had slid into the meeting room just as Terri was gathering those present.

After welcoming the faculty, Terri invited me forward to share. Knowing how I was struggling with my balance, Kelly approached the wooden podium with me and stood at my side as I shared. Looking out at so many of the faces who'd stood with us throughout our difficult season, her post beside me was a beautiful metaphor for the steadfast support she and our community had provided for months. Since speaking words to a roomful of faces was second nature to me, I hadn't anticipated becoming emotional while sharing. So I was surprised to choke up before speaking a single word as I stared down at my phone between glances around the room.

Kelly laid a gentle hand on my back as I attempted to regain my composure.

When I was able to gather myself, I began by reading Psalm 62:8, "Trust in him at all times, you people; pour out your hearts to him, for God is our refuge." I continued by sharing about my early misdiagnosis, when my symptoms had been so easily dismissed. Then, when I shared the unlikely statistical odds of being a healthy thirty-five-year-old with this particular diagnosis—the kind of "anomaly" that no one wants to be—I saw the faces of my friends and acquaintances reflect the pain and agony of that season. I confided in them how I made videos for the girls and Kelly on the night before my surgery to be watched in the event that I didn't make it, and how difficult that was.

But what I was most intent on communicating to these gracious listeners was what I was learning about the pearls and pitfalls of optimism and how it had impacted so much of my journey to that point. If I'm honest, I was happy to believe the doctor who'd initially dismissed my symptoms. I'd been sincere when I accidentally told my parents we were lucky to have caught it early. And in so many other moments of buckling down to bear treatments and surgery and medications and therapies, I had buoyantly assumed that I'd be able to power through it all and return to a life that was a lot like the one I'd been living. Without ever pausing to consider whether that was true or whether the clinical evidence supported it, I clung to my optimism to help sustain me through crises.

I went on to share how I've always been an optimist, so much so—probably to a fault—that Kelly and I often jokingly refer to the way I view, experience, and live in the world as "pathologically optimistic." My optimism wasn't truly *pathological*—compulsive or diseased—but it wasn't always helpful and sometimes wasn't grounded in what was most solid and real. Because research does show that optimism fosters resilience, trying to keep a positive attitude was beneficial to me while facing challenges. But sometimes the optimism to which I'd clung was grounded neither in science—nothing in the medical journals about my odds of surviving were cause for optimism—nor on faith. My natural wiring and lifelong insistence that things would turn out well had helped me peel myself off the mat each time a new phase of my cancer battle and treatment had nearly knocked me out. It had helped me stay in the fight until this point. Without it, I would have surely already thrown in the towel. But with each passing day I was starting to realize that I needed something more than optimism to endure the fight and rounds ahead. Optimism wasn't going to be enough this time.

Though at the time I was giving this devotional I couldn't see it, sometimes my optimism kept me from living in the *now*. Specifically, it prevented me from being truthful with others or myself about how bad things really were. My fellow collaborators and I had studied West Virginia's 2010 Upper Big Branch Mine Explosion. We discovered that family members who remained optimistic during the first several hours of a rescue operation actually hindered the beginning stages of their healing process. What helped many manage their emotions for a while eventually elicited angry, destructive, and even violent reactions when it was dashed by the announcement that none had survived.

And because I had clung to optimism over realism, I'd robbed others, especially Kelly, of owning the reality of what they were going through.

I went on to admit that my illness had challenged that optimism to the point where it no longer held up. Optimism hadn't spared me the physical pain I'd been forced to endure. It hadn't kept me from emotional suffering. It hadn't protected me from what would be lifelong consequences of a surgery that had forever altered my body. And when optimism failed, my entire worldview had been called into question.

And yet as a result, I discovered something even more robust: *hope*. Until this point in life I had often thought of and used the terms "optimism" and "hope" pretty much interchangeably, and I realized I had been wrong in doing so.

To illustrate my own shift in understanding that had been birthed when optimism failed, I shared a thought from Catholic priest, theologian, and pastoral caregiver Henri Nouwen:

> Optimism and hope are radically different attitudes. Optimism is the expectation that things . . . will get better. Hope is trust that God will fulfill God's promises to us in a way that leads us to true freedom. The optimist speaks about concrete changes in the future. The person of hope lives in the moment with the knowledge and trust that all of life is in good hands.

Another way to say it would be that optimism, believing things will be okay in this life, is a *finite* perspective; on the other hand, hope, trusting that if not in this lifetime then in the next God will make things right, is an *eternal* perspective.

Even though I admitted that I hadn't given up my insistent optimism, I slowly started to embrace something different, something even better: hope. I was learning that *hope* was what allowed me to trust God moment by moment, with the confidence that I was in good hands. Hope hadn't meant that I would survive my surgery. Hope didn't even mean I was guaranteed to walk any of my daughters down the aisle if this is where their paths took them. Hope simply meant that I had confidence that my life, my wife's life, and my daughters' lives were in reliable hands. It meant that, moment by moment, I knew I could trust in the One whose love and care and presence did not fail.

To a roomful of people who trusted in a God who was good, I admitted that the shift was a big one for me. It had challenged me to find refuge in God, and to rest in his reliable presence. Nothing about that came naturally to me, but at the end of my own resources, I knew I had been graciously received by One who could be trusted. I told my colleagues that I'd have scans done in May and that, no matter the results, I would still be hanging onto hope that wasn't dependent on scan results or life expectancy.

When I got to the end of my notes, I became aware of how much the brief message had taken out of me. Kelly helped steady me as my legs grew weak. At the suggestion of another professor, my colleagues gathered around me and laid hands on me to pray. Glancing around the circle, I couldn't help but notice all the blue bracelets, the same ones that my colleague had made as signs of solidarity. I was overcome by the holy prayers of those who knew me well and those who did not. My faith was strengthened by brothers and sisters who shared my hope in a God that they, and I, knew to be most certainly *good*.

Because it had taken so much of my energy to make it to the retreat and share with the group, I was wiped out after my friends prayed for me. With regrets, I said good-bye and let Kelly drive me back home, where I was looking forward to collapsing into bed.

Closing my eyes during the short drive, I thought about the work of my friend Roger Sandberg, who has led emergency relief operations for a variety of NGOs. I remembered Roger saying that the two attributes he most often encounters among those displaced in conflict are "acceptance" and "hope." While strange bedfellows at first blush, Roger names them as two sides of the same coin. Acceptance is the recognition that an external event—a war, an earthquake, a typhoon—has created a great loss. And hope is the confidence that, despite all outward signs that beg otherwise, things will one day be different than they are today.

As I meditated on what Roger had learned, I realized I was discovering that optimism alone, or a buoyant confidence in a successful outcome, is too flimsy to allow for real flourishing. My experience had been teaching me what Roger had witnessed: remaining hopeful about the future helps people persist even when life has been turned upside down.

Many of the Syrian refugees Roger had met in settlements in Lebanon still carried their house keys in their pockets. For them, those keys symbolized a resilient hopefulness about the future. They didn't hold onto their keys because they thought their homes would still be standing or because they thought life would return to the way it had been before the mortar rounds started falling. Rather, he writes that they carried their keys as "a constant reminder of hope: hope to return home, hope for their children, and hope for peace." His words echoed those of German theologian Jürgen Moltmann: "Genuine hope is not blind optimism. It is hope with open eyes, which sees the suffering and yet believes in the future."

Releasing the blind optimism to which I'd once clung, I was looking toward the future with more open and hopeful eyes.

As Kelly turned onto President Street, I thought about those house keys and I thought about all the blue bracelets I saw on the outstretched wrists of my colleagues who, just minutes earlier, had placed their hands on me as they prayed. I thought about the blue bracelet that I wore, that I never took off, that symbolized my hope to someday return home, my hope for my children and my wife, and my hope to experience peace once again.

A Year of Drought

When Resilience Isn't Enough

"ONE OF THE nurses mentioned how resilient you are when I brought you up at the doctor's office."

I was reading the email on my phone in bed. It was from a friend of a friend who was receiving oncology treatments at the same facility where I was being treated. They were words I'd heard frequently. Students, colleagues, neighbors, church members all seemed to sound the same chorus: "You're so resilient." And yet every time I heard them, they didn't ring as being true for me. To be fair, I'm sure I'd said the same thing to others. Our culture celebrates a resilience in which survivors bounce right back to the lives they were living before disaster struck. It's exactly how I'd understood resilience as well. But nothing about my experience was particularly springy. Slogging? Yes. Bouncing? No.

I thanked the sender for thinking of me without agreeing to the false premise.

I knew the kind of people who were described as resilient: A former student who was thrust into a coma for six months as a result of a rare disease recovered and bounced off to grad school. A professor who was one of the country's leading forgiveness researchers who was able to go on and forgive the man that murdered his mother. A girl with no legs grew up to perform as an aerialist with Britney Spears' World Tour and is now a bestselling author and sought-after speaker. Those were the kind of spirited characters who embodied resilience.

While I wanted to be that elastic guy who made others feel good by not being overcome by death's sting, the label "resilient" did not feel like the right fit. I don't know what would describe the painful daily process of soldiering on whether I felt like it or not, but it did not feel anything like what resilience should be.

When I'd been diagnosed the previous summer, Kelly had just begun a master's program to earn her degree in nurse midwifery, alongside her part-time job as an assistant in a home birth midwifery practice. The decision—before our lives were turned inside out by cancer—hadn't been an easy one for our family. Kelly's schedule was already unpredictable. And my work as a professor and head of the school's Humanitarian Disaster Institute sometimes required I drop everything and go into full-blown emergency response mode. Occasionally that meant deploying, and other times it meant a blur of writing, consulting, media, and outreach efforts. Kelly and I hadn't made the decision for her to return to school lightly. We knew that getting our three girls to various schools, clubs, practices, lessons, and play dates would require carefully orchestrated teamwork. But we both agreed that Kelly's personal and professional development was worth stretching to accommodate.

Once I was diagnosed, Kelly and I were forced to consider the possibility of her stepping back from school. Kelly had a very strong sense of God's calling to do the work she was doing, as well as the training to advance professionally. And although neither of us wanted to think about it, she was keenly aware of the strong possibility that within a year's time she might become a single parent to our girls and have to provide for them all financially.

When Kelly got home that afternoon, I was out cold in our bedroom upstairs. Quietly slipping back into the house as I napped, she made her way to the study, picked up her Bible, and started searching for a verse she'd recalled hearing. Suddenly it had a gravitational force. Praying, she asked God to help her discern the way forward.

Startled from my snooze, Kelly was already herding the girls through their afterschool routine, helping them organize themselves for homework, evening chores, and working to get dinner on the table. Amid a tornado of talking and laughter and crashing of lunch boxes and backpacks, I hauled myself out of bed and slowly made my way down the stairs. I saw Carlee bounce through our foyer at the bottom of the stairs a few times and then cartwheel through once in the time it took me to walk down twelve brown creaky steps. After making it down the stairwell, I shuffled and plopped onto our blue IKEA couch. Kelly was picking up some homework papers off the living room coffee table.

"Has anyone seen my homework?" Chloe hollered from the kitchen.

"In my hand," Kelly said, then turned her attention back to me.

Colleen stood in the doorway with a paper and pen in hand.

"Can someone sign my permission slip to go to the Field Museum?"

Although I couldn't contribute all I wanted to the household, I was confident I could wiggle a pen.

"I got it, sweetie," I told her. She handed me the pen and paper, and I scribbled what would have to pass as a signature at the bottom of the form.

"Thanks, Dad," she said, before heading up the stairs to her bedroom.

"Can we talk in my study for a sec?" Kelly asked me.

"Sure," I answered, curious.

Slowly moving to an upright position, I stood and walked across the room to the guest room Kelly had been using as an office since she'd started school.

"I found verse in Jeremiah that I wanted to show you," she said.

Tugging her Bible out of her backpack, amid a mound of textbooks and a stack of medical journal articles, Kelly continued, "It's from Jeremiah 17, and it says, 'Blessed is the one who trusts in the Lord, whose confidence is in him. They will be like a tree planted by the water that sends out its roots by the stream. It does not fear when heat comes;

its leaves are always green. It has no worries in a year of drought and never fails to bear fruit'" (Jer. 17:7–8).

Between the chemo-brain, having just woken up, and being distracted by our kids running around, I asked her to read it again.

After reading the verse again, she went on to offer, "I think it means that even though things are really rough right now, it's important for me to still be productive and fruitful. I think I may need to keep doing what I'm doing. I don't think I'm supposed to drop everything."

It was apparent how the words had spoken to Kelly's heart. In the midst of our family's most difficult season, she *was* thriving in so many ways. She took care of me; she loved on our children; she worked crazy, unpredictable hours; she tackled a challenging grad program. It was hard, but she did it. And I'd seen that it was both rewarding and life-giving for her.

I suspected I could predict how Jeremiah's words would guide Kelly. And the promise God gave to his hurting people through the lips of Jeremiah was also speaking to me. Yes, our family was living through a dry season. But that didn't mean that there wasn't a way to be fruitful in the midst of it.

"Kelly, that really resonates as being true for you. And you know I'm supportive of whatever you choose."

Kelly and I both stepped back into the living room when we heard her cell phone ring. She took a deep breath and pivoted back toward the study. I could tell from her voice she was talking to a mother-to-be and was likely getting called out to assist with a birth after another long day.

Realizing Kelly was probably leaving, I moved to the kitchen and started a fresh pot of coffee, knowing she probably had a late night ahead. Carlee hugged me and then bounced off, Chloe was doing her homework at the kitchen counter, and Colleen was reading Harry Potter at the dining room table.

"Sounds like a baby is on its way!" Kelly announced with a smile. I'm taking my textbooks and laptop in case there's any downtime. Text me if you need anything. I've got to run. Wait, are you going to be okay with the girls by yourself tonight?"

"I'm good," I assured her. "Hope you have a good birth. We will be fine."

Kelly started to hustle out the back door after checking in with each of the girls and giving them a hug and kiss good-bye. I caught her to give her a travel mug of coffee right as she was exiting the house onto our back porch.

Grabbing my own Bible, I opened it up to the passage Kelly had shared.

My eyes fell on the end of the passage: "It has no worries in a year of drought and never fails to bear fruit" (Jer. 17:8).

Although on most days I felt useless, unable to produce even a fraction of what I once could, I thought back to a moment a few months before when Typhoon Haiyan had hit the Philippines. As one of the strongest land-falling tropical cyclones on record, Haiyan killed at least sixty-three hundred people. I was only three weeks past my surgery, recovering in bed, and even though I still felt like I'd been run over by a Mack truck, I had managed to prop up my laptop on pillows to craft an op-ed piece for *Christianity Today* titled "How Churches Can Help without Hurting after Super Typhoon Haiyan." Some of the recommendations I shared came from what I had learned from others helping our family through cancer. It was published within hours of submission. Nine hundred twenty-seven words. Those 927 words, though, were the ripe little offering of fruit that I was able to produce during our drought.

Kelly ended up being gone most of the night for work, but she had texted me before I went to sleep to check in on the girls and me. Later the next night, we considered how to best move forward. Although continuing to work, parent the girls, and take care of me as she attended school made for a very full schedule, Kelly was energized by the opportunity to be doing meaningful work and learning. In the end, we both agreed that Kelly pressing forward with school was the right choice for our family. Kelly continuing to grow as a person was actually going to continue to fill her and allow her to become the kind of woman who could live out her multifaceted purpose in the world.

As our family tried to keep living amid our drought, we were forced to reconsider the kind of buoyant resilience we'd been conditioned to value. As a professor I'd always explained it to my classes using the illustration of a beach ball being submerged under pool water, asking, "What eventually happens to the beach ball?" "It bounces back," they'd chime. I could also count on at least one student to follow with, "You have to hop out of the pool to retrieve it!" My students understood that the more positive reserve we have—the way we see the world; our beliefs, habits, and sense of community—the harder it is for the unexpected to keep us down. But going through a disaster or a personal crisis is sometimes more akin to that ball landing on a nail that causes all the air to be expelled almost instantly. While acknowledging the complexities of those punctures, I'd assure my students that a lot of people have the capability to be patched back up and eventually bounce back. That is what resilience looks like.

At the same time, I had seen disasters strike with such force that some people weren't able to bounce back quickly or even be patched back up. Katrina hovered over land as a hurricane for a devastating twenty-three hours before being downgraded to a tropical storm. As soon as the storm passed, everyone who made it through alive was now a survivor. My cancer had been hovering over me since my June diagnosis and was continuing to pound my body. No matter how much I prayed, there was no downgrading the catastrophe in which I found myself.

I had started to wrestle with my understanding of resilience. As someone who was still in the middle of the storm, there was not yet an opportunity for me to bounce back. I knew that as my recovery progressed I was going to need resilience. But Jeremiah's stream-side tree reminded me that, perhaps even more than resilience, *endurance* was what I needed most. I had put my life on hold when cancer struck. I had gone all in with resilience, had done all

I could to push through suffering to get back to the life I once had. It had helped initially, but now I found myself depleted and running on fumes. If I was going to still bear fruit, I was going to have to learn to live in the suffering.

Early in my career I worked on a trauma advisory board for a Christian nonprofit that had developed a program to help women survivors of gender-based violence in the Democratic Republic of the Congo (DRC). Through this work I learned about the people of Goma, a town in the eastern region of the DRC. Although they didn't bounce back from their disaster like a rubber ball, the people of Goma demonstrated steadfast endurance. Goma is a town precariously situated about a dozen miles from Nyiragongo, the world's most active volcano. When Nyiragongo erupted in 2002, the lava exploding from its center reached all the way to Goma, leaving one hundred people dead and over one hundred thousand homeless. Today, large piles of volcanic rock litter Goma's geography. While most of the debris is useless, residents of Goma have used broken pieces of the hardened volcanic stone to make fences. The fences, built of the stacked, jagged, rocklike formations, resemble stone fences in the northeastern United States, where one smooth stone is stacked upon the next. Less expensive than either brick or cement, the debris has also been used to build roads and even bricks for homes. Year after year the people of Goma demonstrate endurance as they rebuild their lives with the with the remnants of the lava flow that shattered their lives.

Years later our team interviewed Congolese refugee

women survivors of sexual violence about how they had coped, including those from Goma. The theme of endurance undergirded many of the stories they entrusted us with as they described how they *and their faith* survived horrific atrocities. I'll never forget what one woman shared with my students who interviewed her as she described how prayer had helped sustain her.

She offered, "I think of God because my heart is in his hands, and because I have my family that remained."

I didn't know if I was going to have enough strength to endure cancer. Reflecting on these brave women's stories I was once again reminded, and finally starting to understand, that maybe it was okay if I didn't meet society's definition of resilience. Cancer had robbed me of most of my physical, mental, emotional, and even spiritual strength. But I still had God and my family, and many others who loved me. I knew there's no such thing as a "self-made" success story, even though our individualistic society clings onto this narrative. Ultimately others contribute to our success, and if I was going to be a survivor success story, I knew in this moment I'd owe such a victory to the strength of those around me. Could it be possible that, as with those Congolese women, if my story didn't unfold the way I hoped it would, I might still experience well-being? It wasn't a thought, though, that I wanted to dwell on too long.

In that season, my family discovered that, in addition to resilience, *endurance* was what I needed in the long run. Endurance is what's needed when you can't see a light at the end of the tunnel. It's those live roots Jeremiah described that stretch out toward a stream, accessing deep nourishment that can sustain life during a drought. It is a strength that does not depend on our own buoyancy but is deeper than ourselves. I'd spent my career studying conventional definitions of resilience that had simply not described my experience. Focusing on endurance and not just resilience was a gift because it helped me let go of feeling like I was failing because I wasn't bouncing back and helped me start to grasp onto the kind of deep-rooted endurance that produced fruit when the land was barren. Most importantly, I learned that being productive didn't always involve doing. Sometimes what others need from us most is to just be. Like, being there to listen to Kelly's day when she got home from work. Or being there to curl up with my daughters when they needed comfort.

Although our lives were definitely messy, we'd discovered that as grounded, rooted people we could be fruitful, even in the desert. What began as Kelly's tree—well, technically Jeremiah's tree—became a symbol for our family of the kind of endurance, in the driest seasons, that produces fruit. And soon it was a symbol for our whole family of the deep resources that could be available to sustain us, even in a drought.

When God Sends a Helicopter

Understanding Spiritual Surrender

ONE MORNING, while still in the midst of chemo, as I lay on my side in bed, it took most of my strength to prop my iPad up to read the personal and work emails that had stacked up over the previous few days. Two of them were from Christian friends, one from church and one from the college, who were thanking God for getting me through surgery and treatments. Though I knew I should be grateful, I wasn't feeling it. And while I wish I could report that I joined their prayers of gratitude, my response was markedly different.

Hey, I thought pridefully, *I'm the one doing the heavy lifting here.*

I was the one who'd soldiered through surgery. I was the one suffering the devastating effects of ongoing treatment. I was the one who could pass out or vomit with little warning. What was there to thank *God* for? It seemed to me that divine intervention might have spared me the indignity and pain I'd been bearing for months.

No sooner had the haughty thought forced its way into

my consciousness than I was convicted by the arrogance and pride that had poisoned my heart. I rattled off a quick apology to God and hauled myself out of bed to see how much snow had fallen the previous night. As I rose I heard Kelly dash out the door downstairs, hustling the girls out the door and into the van to get them to school.

During this season when chemo was zapping the life from me, there were many days when I was physically unable to get out of bed. On these days, the smallest acts of productivity felt like pretty big accomplishments. I felt chronically guilty that I couldn't contribute more to our household.

I'd gradually begun to learn that because I couldn't do everything on my own, I needed to rely on others. While I wish I could say that I was an A+ student in this area, the truth was that I struggled to accept my limitations. When it came to graciously receiving what I needed from others, I was a slow learner.

When I looked out the window at the crisp new snow, still whipping through the sky, I noticed our neighbors had rolled their large blue plastic garbage and recycling buckets to the curb. While no part of me wanted to step outside into the below-freezing temperatures of a Chicago winter, I knew that accomplishing the simple household chore would be a win for me and for my family.

Letting my own weight drag me down the staircase, I grabbed my black button-up winter coat from the mudroom. I put on my thick wool winter socks and laced up my black waterproof hiking winter boots. As I was making my way through the house to the door, I caught a glimpse of myself in the mirror. My thick red hair had started falling out in clumps. I'd had Kelly shave my head with a pair of hair clippers, leaving just enough length to not be considered bald. I felt like I was teaching cancer a lesson: I couldn't stop the chemotherapy from taking my hair in patches and strands, but I could control when and how I was going to lose the rest of it. I put on my black and dark gray toboggan to keep my newly buzzed head warm. I reached into my pockets for my black winter leather gloves and pulled them over my hands. Then I wrapped my black fleece Nike swoosh scarf around my neck and covered my face. I would have looked like I was gearing up to commit a crime had it not been for my blue flannel pajama pants. Bracing myself while I opened the door, I stepped out into the elements. The crackle of icy snow crunched under my boots, and bitter winds whipped against me.

While the weather would have felt biting to anyone who faced it that day, the treatments I was receiving made my body painfully sensitive to cold. The abrasiveness of icy flakes hitting my cheeks, each gust of wind on my hands and feet, felt like I was being cut by tiny razors as I pulled the trash and recyclables down our long driveway. And although I resisted gulping in the cold air, I was physically spent by the time I neared the curb. When my scarf slipped off my face just as I was inhaling to catch my breath, it felt like I was swallowing broken glass.

"God *heal* me," I begged spontaneously. "Please heal me, take this from me . . ."

As I finished lining up the large plastic bins beside the street, I became aware of the prayer that had burst forth, unauthorized, from my depths. The doctors had been doing all they could do. My family and friends had been doing all they could do. I had been doing all I could do. I just wanted the pain to stop. I wanted the fear to go away. I wanted the episodes of unexpected crying to go away. I wanted the cancer gone. Desperate words and prayers continued to fill my heart and mind as I started walking toward the house with my last bit of energy.

After "hearing" the deep cry of my heart for relief from physical and emotional suffering, I became aware of an internal monologue unfolding inside me.

Does God even hear me?

Does God answer prayers?

Is it right for me to ask for healing?

If God does hear me, will God do anything?

Is there even a God?

Surprised and rattled by my own musings, I felt alarmed by the question that had arisen. Fearful, eager to silence the unauthorized intruder, I shifted from "sufferer" mode to "researcher" mode.

Statistically speaking, I reasoned silently as I passed the two giant pine trees in our front yard, *praying has been associated with improved mortality odds and a greater sense of well-being. . . .* So, I decided to keep praying, even though I was plagued by questions.

The sharp winter air continued to cut through me, as if I had no protection from it. And as I carefully negotiated the icy path back to the house, I recognized the flimsy logic. Yes, I knew that people in crisis pray more and that prayer was linked to better emotional and health indicators. But the rationale skirted the deeper question of my heart: *Was there a loving God who was attentive to my cry and able to help?*

Pushing through the mudroom door, my shivering frame welcomed the warm air as I made my way into the kitchen. Kicking off my snow-covered boots and hanging my coat on a hook, I walked toward the living room. As my body tried to readjust to a reasonable temperature, I became aware that the chore had sapped me. Eyeing the couch in the living room, I wanted nothing more than to crash into it and fall asleep. But I knew that if I could make it upstairs—twelve creaky wooden steps that now stretched before me like twelve *flights* of stairs—I would be better off. The table beside my bedside had my water bottle, pain reliever, books, and iPad. Though I doubted I could accomplish anything more that day, I would be comforted knowing that all I needed would at least be in reach.

Glancing toward our second floor, the climb ahead of me felt no less daunting than scaling Mount Everest. Gripping the handrail, I fought gravity to put one foot in front of the other, climbing to the top of the stairs. After pausing to catch my breath at the top, I skimmed my hand along the wall as I stepped carefully toward our bedroom. I still felt unsettled by the turbulent questions about God's reliability that had flooded my mind in the vulnerable moments I'd ventured outside. I needed to press onward.

Putting one arm on our bed's footboard and one on the

mattress to support some of my weight, I suddenly and unexpectedly dropped to my knees beside the bed Kelly and I shared and continued to pray. Purposing to shut off the part of my brain that wanted to understand and control God, I allowed the deep, uncensored, primal prayers of my heart to rise up, offering them in all their nakedness to God.

I spit out the prayer that had first burst forth from the excruciating, knifelike pain I'd felt outside: "God, take this from me." And yet as I continued to open my heart honestly before God, I noticed that the prayer gave way to another: "If I'm not okay, please take care of my wife and my daughters."

I knew Christians who'd never utter a prayer like the one I'd mouthed. Their fierce insistence on faith in God left no room for doubt, almost bullying God to prove himself as a healer. Yet I also knew that the Scriptures were saturated with themes of spiritual surrender: "Whoever wants to save their life will lose it" (Matt. 16:35); "See, we have left all and followed you" (Mark 10:28); "You were taught, with regard to your former way of life, to put off your old self . . . to be made new" (Eph. 4:22–23). But my experience of spiritual surrender had been complicated by some Christians insisting on their own way that felt more like "putting the LORD your God to the test" (Deut. 6:16) than any kind of faith in the Divine. I knew if these believers had been able to eavesdrop on my prayer, they would have counted it against me, as if I did not have enough faith for God to work with.

But that wasn't my experience. To me, it felt *more* faithful to allow both that I didn't know what God's will was and also that I couldn't manipulate God to do my bidding. In that moment I had the deep sense that I could trust God *regardless* of the outcome. I knew that, in my absence, God could and would care for the four people I loved more than anything in the world.

On that frigid, icy morning, my desperate begging for mercy had given way to a deeper, more robust reliance on God. And as I felt my heart rate return to normal, my breathing become more regular, I became aware that if, in this finite life, I was not okay, God could still be trusted. I knew beyond a shadow of a doubt that I could trust God with my health, my life, and my family. I could choose to be confident in God even when I could not predict the outcome of my struggle.

A deep sense of peace washed over me. Desperate clawing and bargaining and pleading had been replaced with a quiet confidence in God's goodness and reliability that was not dependent on the outcome for which I hoped. Noticing my aching knees, I hoisted myself back to a standing position and rolled into bed. Pulling a soft, fleecy blanket over my body, my researcher brain clicked back into gear as two words that identified what I'd just experienced landed forcefully in my heart: *spiritual surrender.*

Years earlier I'd researched the benefits of spiritual surrender on survivors of Hurricane Katrina. Our discoveries—that those who engaged in spiritual surrender viewed God more positively and could release more control to

God—resonated with other research proving that those who shared that view of God, on the whole, tended to fare better psychologically.

At the time, though, I had viewed spiritual surrender as a passive act. Quite frankly, it smacked of all the makings of a twangy country song. I couldn't help but think of "Jesus, Take the Wheel" (sorry Carrie Underwood fans). In the song, a woman is driving to her folks' home in Cincinnati on Christmas Eve, with her infant daughter sleeping in the backseat. She loses control and her vehicle spins across a patch of black ice. In that moment, as she sees their lives flash before her eyes, she throws her hands up in the air and says, "Jesus, take the wheel." Once safely on the side of the road, she cries out, "I'm sorry for the way I've been living my life. I know I've got to change." She goes on to ask Jesus this time to take the "wheel" of her life. I could relate to the later example of surrender and putting trust in Jesus. But the literal throwing up of her hands in the air when she still had a role to play in trying to protect herself and child concerns me. Like those who had seemingly tried to bully God's will in step with theirs, negating any personal responsibility seemed to me another example of putting God to the test.

That resistance to extreme surrender is exactly what I'd assumed about the research findings on spiritual surrender. I was more likely to associate "surrender" with the waving a white flag in the face of life's difficulties than something truly spiritual. Like a parent who refuses to seek medical attention for their child because they have prayed God would heal their child.

Honestly, it reminded me of the classic disaster-rescue folktale of a man in need of rescue as the floodwaters rose. When volunteers with a rescue truck knocked on the front door of his home to save him, he refused, saying, "God will save me." When the next round of heroes came by in boats, he again refused rescue, insisting, "God will save me." The last attempt to save the man was a helicopter dipping down to assist the man in getting off of his roof. Shouting up at the helicopter, he continued to argue, "God will save me." When the man dies in the flood, he shows up at the Pearly Gates a little perturbed, demanding to know why God hadn't saved him. God, equally irritated, answered, "I sent a truck, a boat, and a helicopter! What more did you want?" In my worst moments, that kind of hardheaded refusal to participate in one's own redemption was the negative spin I'd assigned to spiritual surrender.

That said, I recognize that this particular spiritual notion hit a nerve for me. Having grown up in a small, rural farming community, where so many people's livelihoods were dependent on the elements—where flooding could wipe out unharvested crops and oil drying up could lead to job layoffs. When I was a kid, it often felt to me like life was happening to *us*. At the same time, I grew up in a community where the Puritan work ethic still ran strong.

I'd grown up and chosen a life where self-advocacy and determination could be efficacious in changing one's situation. I thought if I earned the right degrees, published the right research, and built the right relationships, I might be able to create life and sense of security I sought. I didn't want to feel so dependent on factors I couldn't control. And while I understood that the data on the benefits of spiritual surrender proved that it worked for many, I frankly struggled with the idea.

What I learned on my knees beside our bed, though, when I'd come completely to the end of myself, was that nothing was passive about spiritual surrender. It was by far the hardest prayer I've ever prayed in my life. Deciding to trust God when the outcome of that choice was unpredictable was a willful act of obedience.

I now understood the difference between spiritual surrender and counterfit expressions of surrender I had too often confused for the real thing.

And as I'd continued to consider the relationship between optimism and hope, I realized that genuine hope required surrender. For hope to be authentic, for it to be a sturdy hope that transcended earthly optimism, it depended upon spiritual surrender.

Comforted by the gentle weight of the blanket over me, my thoughts gave way to the insistence of slumber. Resting in a new confidence, I let my heavy lids close. And as I drifted off to sleep, I still didn't know if things were going to be okay. But for the first time since hearing, "It's cancer," I experienced a strong sense of peace that my family and I were in good hands.

CHAPTER 13

After the Storm Passes

Finding Your New Normal

I F I COULD just make it through surgery, it would all be over. That's what I'd thought in the fall. But it wasn't over, because the doctor prescribed chemotherapy treatments for safe measure.

If I could just make it through my last chemo treatment, I told myself, *it would be over.* But during chemo I realized that I'd need some sort of scan to verify that there was no evidence of disease.

If I could just make it through the scan to verify that I was well, it would all be over.

Then I found out I had to wait two weeks from my last treatment to get scanned and get the results.

If I can just make it another two weeks, then, finally, it would all be over.

This was the "if . . . then" logic I clung to throughout my cancer journey.

After I'd received my last chemotherapy treatment at the cancer center, the nurses who had helped care for me celebrated my wellness with balloons and a slice of cake while gleefully singing "Happy Last Day of Chemo," a song I'm assuming they had made up, to the tune of "Happy Birthday." Kelly and I kissed in celebration and had the nurses take a picture of us together in my treatment room to document that we had finally reached the end of my treatments.

I felt a bit self-conscious as Kelly and I left the office because of all the folks in the waiting room without balloons and cake. I quietly hoped that the jubilant display would encourage and inspire those hoping for their own eventual celebrations. As we headed for the elevators I remembered sitting in that very space on my first day of chemo. I recalled that a frail elderly woman, wearing a brightly colored bandana to disguise her hair loss, had just completed her final day of chemo. I must have looked nervous and scared as I anticipated the unknown because she stopped and shared her good news with me and gave me a hug before walking out.

We knew we'd have to wait two weeks for the scan results that would determine whether I was truly cancer-free. Optimists would call this "remission," but cautious pessimists would only concede "no evidence of disease." Months earlier my mom had mentioned to our girls that she wanted to celebrate in a special way when we received word that I didn't have cancer. She'd asked the girls what she should do to celebrate, and without hesitating, Chloe exclaimed, "A cartwheel!" Pretty sure that's not what my mother had in mind. As we headed toward the car, I smiled at the thought that we all could be celebrating in just a few weeks.

The last round of chemotherapy had left me feeling worn out and weak. But I felt something I hadn't felt in a long time: excitement—the sort of excitement I experienced as a kid trying not to fall asleep the night before Christmas in hopes of catching a peak at Santa Claus delivering the blue remote-control truck I so desperately wanted. I had waited for this day for so long, and now it was here. I couldn't wait to get home and tell the girls, "Daddy is done with chemo!" Kelly and I discussed how happy we were to be done and laughed at the song the nurses had sung and about how excited I was to tell the girls the good news. But like a child waiting up past his bedtime for Santa, exhaustion from six months of chemo made it hard to keep my eyes open. Kelly encouraged me to lean the car seat back and rest so that I'd have some energy to see our girls once we got home.

I heard the turn signal as Kelly pivoted into the driveway and slowly came to as the car slowed to a stop. As Kelly and I walked into the kitchen through the screen door, I realized that the girls already knew. No sooner had we stepped through the door than our three little redheads gleefully jumped out, throwing handfuls of home-cut confetti in the air while they danced around us yelling, "Surprise!"

The smiles on Kelly's and their trusted babysitter, Miranda's, faces signaled that they were in the know, which was confirmed when I saw a beautiful cake on the kitchen table. The white sheet cake featured an image of a solidly planted tree whose roots sank deep—the image from Jeremiah 17 that had come to mean so much to our family.

Long after the confetti had been tossed, the girls continued to dance in circles around the kitchen. Seeing the pure joy on my girls' faces was one of the most satisfying moments I've ever experienced. All of the pain and loss I'd endured—in the name of "treatment"!—was worth it for that moment alone.

Later that night after I had tucked Colleen and Carlee into bed, I dipped into Chloe's room. Sitting down on her My Little Pony bedspread, I picked up her stuffed panda named Violet. We read a story together, which Violet also enjoyed, and then Chloe kicked her leg out from under her covers, displaying the blue rubber bracelet on her ankle.

"Dad," she assured me authoritatively, "now that you are done, I can take this off."

When my colleague Michael had the bracelets made that said, "Lord hear our prayers," Chloe had insisted on wearing one until I was well. Because the adult-size bracelet slid down her narrow arms past her elbow, she'd worn it as an anklet. Truly, she never took it off. She bathed with it on, she swam with it on, she slept with it on. The strong sense of confidence she was displaying was signature Chloe Aten. Her childlike faith caused me to well up with emotion.

"Chloe," I said, "I think that's a great idea."

With a big grin, Chloe removed the anklet she'd worn for almost a year and laid it on her nightstand. And with that ceremonial placement, it was official: I was well. Life had returned to normal.

Except that it hadn't.

Physically I was not the same as I'd been before cancer. Over the next few months, I slowly started to get some energy and strength back. Not much, but some. And now my body carried the memory of the physical traumas it endured during almost a year's worth of treatments. Sometimes my body's fight-or-flight reflex would kick in out of nowhere. It could be as mundane as getting a work email alerting me to an unanticipated schedule change while working on another project. Instead of feeling like a minor detour in my day, my body responded like a white-knuckled driver does when seeing a wreck unfold a couple of cars ahead in her lane: my heart rate jumped, arousal signals went into overdrive, muscles tensed, and thoughts raced. When the body detects a threat, the autonomic nervous system sounds an alarm, warning that something is wrong. The amygdala, the area of the brain responsible for emotions, memory, and survival instincts, is activated like a gas pedal hitting the floor. Stress hormones are automatically released, triggering an automatic instinctive reaction to danger.

And there were a lot of other changes, too. "Dad, let's go for a bike ride!" my girls invited me one Sunday afternoon. After inflating my tires and adjusting the seat, I mounted my bike and eagerly started to pedal. I immediately toppled over. Beyond my struggles with physical weakness, lasting neuropathy in my feet meant that they remained permanently numb. And because some of one's balance depends on one's feet, I found my numb feet had made it next to impossible for me to balance myself on the bike.

Intellectually I was also not the same as I had been before cancer. My cognitive functioning had been compromised. While I was still receiving treatments, pain was keeping me awake at night. One sleepless night, shortly after starting treatments, I had started thinking about all the manuals I'd written about disaster ministry and realized that I might have a viable book idea. For six and a half hours I cut and pasted material I'd written into the draft of a book. Ideas were flowing! I was really in the zone, making the most of my time and grateful to have something other than my pain to think about. The flurry of work did result in a book contract that I worked hard to complete on other, similar sleepless nights. When I finally received feedback on that first draft, though, I realized that I needed to rewrite almost the entire book. A bit more aware by that point, I finally knew enough to be embarrassed by what I'd first sent.

Unfortunately, the incident wasn't an isolated one. One day I was contacted by a program officer from a foundation to which I had pitched a research grant idea shortly before my cancer. He was emailing to invite my colleagues and me to submit a full proposal for a study on how people make meaning related to God and grow amid natural disasters. Struggling to draft a concept paper to send to my colleagues working on the grant, I admitted, to my collaborators and to myself, that it wasn't my best work. A month later I emailed my fellow collaborators to assure them, "I'm back now! I'm ready to go!" But a few months after that, I realized that what I'd sent them had been subpar. So I had to email them again, saying, "I think now I'm *actually* back. . . ." Because this kept happening, I realized that I'd had no idea how very low functioning I had been. That series of experiences created all kinds of doubt. I didn't trust myself, and I lost confidence in my abilities. It was eight months after my last chemotherapy treatment before I felt like I was finally back in the game mentally.

Emotionally I was not the same as I was before cancer. I continued to struggle with anxiety that cancer would return. While I was grateful that the cancer had been eliminated from my body, and aware that I'd fared better than so many facing the same disease, I lived with the constant awareness that it could return. As a Stage IV cancer survivor, I knew I was considered a high risk for reoccurrence.

One night I was working late, typing away on my laptop at a local coffee shop, when I noticed my back felt uncomfortable as I stretched my hands in the air and yawned. The pain felt like a knot in my right shoulder blade.

Could the cancer be back? Was cancer causing my pain?

I started to panic. I took a few deep breaths, trying to lower the anxiety that seemed to be spreading through every cell of my body. Reaching behind my neck with my right hand, I could feel that it was just some muscle tension causing the discomfort. The thoughts of a cancer reoccurrence slowly started to fade, but my body held onto the anxiety.

Relationally I was not the same as I was before cancer. Sometimes I would get upset about small issues that in the past wouldn't have caused me any concern. One of my favorite sayings has always been, "Let's play it by ear." But now there were moments when I'd go from a fun-loving, spontaneous, "There are lots of ways to do this" dad to suddenly being a rigid, inflexible, "You need to do it this way because I said so" dad. Other times I'd perceive small disagreements between Kelly and me as arguments and end up fighting nonexistent fights. And even though I had missed my friends and colleagues, I often isolated myself, turning down invites to hang out or share a meal.

My *self-image* was not the same as it was before cancer. The first time I saw an old friend after being declared well, he marveled, "Jamie, you must feel invincible after surviving everything you've been through and finding out there's no cancer, right?" His cell phone rang before I could answer, and the question was left hanging. Even though no words left my mouth before his phone rang, the words that pounded in my head were, *No, if anything I feel more fragile than ever.*

Any time someone asked if I might get a tattoo to commemorate my victory over cancer, I would joke that I was afraid that combining tattoos with the surgery scars would make me too intimidating of a figure. But in reality, I'd become self-conscious about my body. Though I knew people couldn't tell I had a colostomy from just looking at me, I always wore an untucked button-up shirt because they tended to fit more loosely and were made of thicker material, which disguised the silhouette of my colostomy bag. And I was thankful for cooler weather, so I had an excuse to wear a jacket or sport coat. Then there were the multiple hernias around my stomach area that had developed, which caused my stomach to protrude in an odd shape. I was still getting to know my new body.

Spiritually I was not the same as I was before cancer. Thinking I was on the other side of cancer's effects, the sense of refuge I'd found in God was slowing fading as the urgent threat passed. The way I experienced and understood God had been inverted: I knew God more deeply but held my theology more lightly. Some beliefs I thought had been essential to my faith were now nonessential and vice-versa. Certain beliefs that were once clearly black-or-white were now gray. I found I connected to God more through liturgy now than through receiving teaching and preaching, which was another one of those reversals. I also found it difficult to be engaged in worship, given my new physical and emotional limitations: standing on numb feet made me ache; being still allowed my anxiety to surface; being pummeled by intrusive questions that only a doctor should ask caused me to withdraw from others; fearing I'd have a problem with my colostomy or that someone would notice my hernia caused me to focus on insecurities instead of God.

Life was different after having faced death squarely for

so long. As much as I wanted to believe that the coming of "no evidence of disease" day would mean that I would cross the finish line and everything would return to normal, I was just starting to realize that there were more legs to the race.

For nearly a year I'd been like someone stuck in a disaster zone who had hid in the basement of his home. As I began to emerge, I expected to find the house I remembered. I expected life to move on as it had before. What I was completely unprepared for, though, was that my house had come close to being knocked down. I was surrounded by debris, shards of the life I'd known. I didn't know where to begin the rebuilding process from the pieces of my old life. One of the toughest realities for disaster survivors— and one with which I now struggled—is that the road to recovery is long and rarely leads back to life as it once was.

When Hurricane Camille hit Mississippi and Louisiana in August 1969, it was purported to be a once-in-a-lifetime disaster. People living in the area never expected to see devastation like Camille in their lifetimes again. They could not have anticipated that in 2005, another hurricane, Katrina, would devastate their state once again. Hurricane Katrina was considered a once-every-hundred-years disaster. Haiti's 2010 earthquake was considered a once-in-five-hundred-years disaster. And Japan's earthquake and tsunami in 2011 were considered a once-in-a-thousand-years disaster. When disaster strikes, we want—more than anything—to believe that it cannot happen again, that it is behind us, that things will return to the way they'd been.

And yet, as it was in Louisiana and Mississippi, there are no guarantees—neither that we will return to normal, nor how long normal might last.

Although I yearned for the life I'd known, I was discovering that little was as it had been. It was time for me to find a new normal.

Two weeks after my girls celebrated the end of chemo, Kelly and I got the good news from Dr. Patel: "no evidence of disease." We called both of our parents on the way home from the cancer center. The next day my phone buzzed with a new text from my dad, who'd sent a photograph of my mom doing a cartwheel in their backyard. The girls giggled in unison when I showed it to them. And, because my mom had pulled a muscle in her leg, the *following* day I received a second text with a picture of her doctor's note, which read, "No more cartwheels."

While I'd eventually regain full cognitive function, my body, heart, and soul were forever changed. No finish line demarcated the end of our journey. Each time I thought there might be, I discovered yet more legs to the race. So, while it was good and right that we celebrated a disease-free body, which I name as one of the happiest moments of my life, I began to realize that there would be new challenges ahead that I couldn't have predicted or anticipated. There was no getting around it—my life was indelibly different.

When I'd first seen the timeline of my life being severed into two parts, "before cancer" and "after cancer," my concern was only how *long* the after-cancer segment of the timeline would be. I hadn't realized that it wasn't just the *length* of the segment that could be altered. Even though I'd successfully made it through all the hoops—the treatments and surgeries and scans—life did not return to what it had once been.

I was living a new normal.

An Epidemic of Fear

Facing Our Mortality

S EVERAL MONTHS before being diagnosed with cancer,,
I was hammering out some work at Blackberry Market. Amid espresso machine sounds and whiffs of the best cinnamon rolls I've eaten filling the air, I glanced up from my laptop and noticed Brett, a Wheaton colleague from the English Department, ducking out of the falling snow through the restaurant's front door. He was a few years older than me, with two kids just a bit older than my girls. I smiled and tilted my head up in a nod, fingers still fixed on my keyboard.

The market was hopping, and Brett scored one of the last open tables adjacent to mine. He set his bag on the booth bench and hung his coat on a nearby hook. Fresh flakes fell to the floor as he paused to greet me.

"Fancy meeting you here," he said with a knowing grin.

Brett and I had both been frustrated by the myriad inter-ruptions when we attempted to write on campus, even in our closed-door offices. He was a poet, and I was writing to make the center's research available and accessible to folks in churches. So when we'd flee campus seeking safe shelter at Blackberry Market or one of the local coffee shops, where the only blessed interruption was a kind server refilling our coffee cups, our paths would often cross at our hideaway locations. I was always happy to see him, feeling emboldened by our shared commitment to writing. To avoid the temptation of polite small talk, we never shared a table.

And yet one of us would often pause for a quick hello, on the way to the restroom or back out the door to grab a highlighter from a car, and we'd start about how we wish we had more time to write, how difficult it was to find blocks of time to write, and how far behind we were on our numerous writing projects. Thirty minutes later one of us would recognize the absurdity—that we'd lost time complaining about not having enough time to write—and we'd each buckle down again.

During the summer of my third year at Wheaton, just weeks into remission, I was in the backyard with my girls. Carlee wanted to play princesses. Chloe wanted to play cowgirls. Colleen wanted to make up and direct a play. We struck a compromise. They were pretending our wooden playhouse structure in the backyard, the one my father helped me build, was a cowgirl castle stage. When I peeked at my phone, I saw that I'd received an email from Brett.

Skimming it quickly, Brett was letting me know he had just been diagnosed with a cancer similar to mine. Stunned, wanting to believe I'd misread it, I reread it more slowly.

"Dad, look at me ride my horse," Chloe begged.

Forcing a smile, I lifted my eyes to admire her riding a pretend Thoroughbred.

How old was Brett's daughter? Though I'd not met her, I remembered she was about a year or so older than Colleen. And was his son in middle school? Or was it the other way around?

"Good job, Princess Cowgirl Chloe!" I methodically praised. "You're doing a great job riding that horse."

Stunned, the backyard merriment faded from my awareness. As the girls continued to play in their land of make-believe, I was singularly focused on the unavoidable reality of what was unfolding for Brett five miles away at Central DuPage Hospital.

"I'm going inside to talk to Mom," I announced to the girls. "I'll be right back."

Walking through the house I found Kelly hard at work in the study just off the living room, working on a paper for graduate school. "Hey, Kel," I began, cracking open the door. "Can you talk for a sec?"

Still undone, I shared Brett's email with her. He'd asked some very specific questions about treatment and was seeking my perspective. As we discussed when I could get over to the hospital to visit, I felt the same rub I'd seen my own loved ones experience. As they had, I wanted to share the "right words." I was, after all, a helping professional trained to discern and speak "right words." But I also knew that there'd be no shortage of professionals, survivors, Googled articles, and well-meaning friends to offer advice similar to what I might offer. Yes, our diagnoses sounded remarkably similar. But what I knew, both professionally and personally, was that what was more useful was to simply be present. To listen well.

Kelly decided to take a break from studying and watch the girls so that I could go see Brett. I drove toward Central DuPage Hospital and noticed my heart rate quicken as memories from my surgery I had there started to flood me. I turned onto Winfield Road toward the hospital. It was one of the few times I had been back to the hospital since my surgery.

After walking toward the hospital entrance, the familiar automated glass doors opened to swallow me up. And though I was confident I'd be spit back out in less than an hour, I was keenly aware of the familiar odor and sounds and sights that once signaled my mortality.

They still did.

Feeling my heartbeat accelerate, I scolded myself for the panic I felt rising inside me.

Jamie, you're fine. No evidence of disease!

Be rational. . . . Just being in the same building as sick people will not make you sick again.

Though at one level I understood all these things to be true, something inside me had clearly been triggered.

Brett's room was on the same wing where I'd recovered after my surgery. Though his door was ajar, I knocked lightly as I entered.

"Come on in!" Brett welcomed. The levity in his voice belied his condition.

Two women were seated beside Brett's bed. I greeted his

wife, Anise, whom I'd met a couple times of before, and Brett introduced me to his mother-in-law.

Brett was in very good spirits. His buoyant likableness was evident, even in his current condition.

I dragged a chair from the far side of the room and joined them.

Brett began, "I've got a lot of questions for you."

Was I really the seasoned expert now? Every moment of my own journey I'd felt like a kindergartner who knew nothing and had to learn everything. I still did.

Brett wanted to know what things had been like, welcoming any advice I might be able to share on practices and doctors, treatments and surgeries.

"You know what I'm going through," he remarked.

I was happy to share what I could but I also knew that his experience would be unique. I could relate to what he was going through, but I had learned that everyone's experience with adversity is distinctively their own. I answered what practical questions I could and marveled at how articulate Brett was, even after just going through the ringer. He went on to share how seeing me doing well spurred a sense of hopefulness in him.

"There will be some similarities," I offered cautiously, "but everyone goes through it differently. So there will be parts of your experience that I don't know."

Our conversation—about sharing the news with our children, and foods that induce nausea, and comfortable clothing to wear to treatments—reminded me what the journey had been like for me. I admitted that I'd also had a plethora of questions and found the whole process to be confusing. My heart ached knowing some of the challenges that may lay ahead for Brett and his family.

When I left the hospital, I noticed stirrings of uneasiness. I was so glad to be a support to Brett in any way I could. But I also noticed a lingering anxiety as I left the hospital and returned to my regular routine.

Come on, Jamie. You're fine . . .

Over the next several months Brett and I got together several times for coffee to talk about battling cancer, our families, and of course writing still found its way into our conversations. Emails were exchanged, and the conversations extended between our get-togethers.

Then connecting got more challenging. For months, Brett and I struggled to find time together. I had a number of trips. Kelly and I were still trying to find a rhythm juggling taking care of our kids during her residency, which required her to be a couple hours away in Rockford several days a week. Some major mandatory work meetings popped up unexpectedly for me, which meant I had to cancel with Brett a few times. As his treatments became harder, there had been a couple times when Brett had not felt up to meeting and needed to cancel as well. Brett had emailed me, and I'd not gotten back to him to nail down a time we could connect.

One afternoon in the midst of spring finals, I was hiding out in Starbucks writing at a table near the glass door entryway. I glanced up when someone approached who seemed to recognize me. I briefly looked up while my fingers finished the last couple of keystrokes in a sentence, only partly shifting my attention from my work. It took a moment for my brain to register that the smiling face coming through the door belonged to Brett. In between a few double-takes, fear fired a warning shot through my body. The terror felt similar to that moment when being startled awake from a bad dream about falling right before crashing into the ground: the body jerks, sleep breaks, eyes open wide, heart pounds, muscles tense, brain races.

Brett and I hadn't connected in person for months, and his face looked so different. His countenance was pale and drawn, cheeks hollow. He'd lost a lot of weight. What looked like an oversized shirt fell loosely over his shoulders, and his jeans were cinched at the waist with a belt that kept them from falling to the ground. Brett's walk revealed fatigue, and his posture showed how weary he was. His hair had thinned. Yet despite his gaunt appearance, Brett was his usual warm self. He introduced me to his friend John Wilson, whom I knew by reputation.

Shocked, I was flooded by fear at the sight of Brett. My stomach sank as I realized that the man I was seeing might just as easily have been me.

"Hey, Brett!" I said, keenly aware of my own girth and trying to disguise my surprise at his deterioration. "I owe you an email!"

Brett and John chatted with me a moment at my table before getting into line, Brett wanting to know how I was doing.

His genuine interest moved me and I was touched by his

authentic interest in me and my family. We had time to exchange the most rudimentary pleasantries when a busy college-aged barista delivered Brett's and John's coffees, at which point we said good-bye as they moved toward an open table.

Clutching my own dark-roast-hold-the-cream coffee, I promised, "I'll shoot you an email with some available times. I really want to catch up."

As they walked toward the back of Starbucks, I was forced to face my own resistance to spending time with Brett. He'd emailed me three weeks earlier, and I'd not responded. I'd soothed my conscious while scrolling through my full inbox by convincing myself that my failure to respond was coming from the right place. When I was in a rush, I told myself that I wanted to give my reply to Brett the time and attention it deserved. I wanted to have just the right words. Wanting to honor him, I'd decide to wait on a reply rather than rush a thoughtless response. That was the logic. I'd also tell myself it was because I had too much work piling up and deadlines I couldn't afford to miss. Kelly was out of town. Or it was because I had a string of meetings lined up for the week already. Or I'd persuade myself that the girls' schedules precluded an evening out that week.

All were true.

But it was also true that I was, myself, anticipating a scan that would reveal whether my own cancer had returned. I'd been feeling anxious about that and wasn't eager to be with the friend whose illness forced me to face my own mortality.

And so, I withdrew.

According to terror management research, we often experience threats to others as a threat to ourselves. Their condition tugs at our existential anxieties, forcing us to face our own mortality. Terror management theory (TMT) explains why people living with HIV-AIDS receive very little human touch, even though the disease can't be transmitted by touch. Our team also found that TMT can even drive our political opinions on issues such as refugees. The pain of others exposes our own. And we manage that terror by avoiding or eliminating the source that triggers our anxiety.

The year I learned I was in remission and Brett received his diagnosis, Thomas Eric Duncan flew from Monrovia, Liberia, to Dallas, with stops in Brussels and Washington, D.C. At the time, East Africa was experiencing an epidemic of the Ebola virus. When Duncan, a native Liberian, began to experience pain, nausea, and dizziness on U.S. soil, he sought care at Texas Health Presbyterian Hospital.

Five days later he was diagnosed with Ebola. A week after that, he was dead.

America panicked.

Though two of the nurses who cared for him contracted the virus, both recovered.

Reacting to the scare, patients stopped visiting Texas Health Presbyterian Hospital. When a doctor in New York was diagnosed with Ebola a few weeks later, an anonymous source reported that nurses were calling in sick to avoid caring for him. Parents in Hazlehurst, Mississippi, kept their children home from school because a principal there had recently visited Zambia for his brother's funeral. To avoid disrupting the children's education, the principal agreed to take personal vacation time despite the fact that Zambia, which isn't even located in western Africa, had no known cases of the disease.

Within weeks of the first Ebola case in the United States, we had surveyed nine hundred people from across the country. One of the things we found was that Ebola served as a reminder of death for people. Ebola had gone from an abstract disease that affects people in other countries to a personal threat made salient in Thomas Eric Duncan's diagnosis. Duncan's illness brought many Americans face-to-face with their own finiteness and mortality. While I'd understood our findings on an intellectual level, running into Brett and John at Starbucks was the first time I understood it in my bones.

Brett remained on my mind for the rest of the day.

That night, as Kelly slept soundly at my side, I watched the red glowing numbers on our clock approach midnight and then cycle well past it. My mind was busy reviewing what I remembered of the research I'd worked on with our team. As it had been so often on my journey, the professional had collided with the personal.

In his 1973 Pulitzer Prize–winning book, *The Denial of Death*, Ernest Becker examines human beings' existential fear of death. Becker argues not that some of our behavior is driven by our fear of death, but that *most* of it is! Choices as seismic as whether to jump out of an airplane to ones as seemingly insignificant as coloring our hair or beards—to preserve the appearance that we are youthful and, ultimately, not dying—are driven by a primal anxiety about death. Becker's theory and TMT research rippled through my conscious and unconscious choices. I knew I'd been dreading the six-month scan that would reveal whether my cancer had returned. I'd been less aware, until bumping into Brett, that I'd been avoiding reminders that made it harder to keep my own mortality at bay.

Even though I'd avoided death's clutches once, I was still scrambling to escape it. Because I'd seen Brett, I was no longer be able to avoid it.

CHAPTER 15

Flooded by Comparison

Coming to Terms with Survivor Guilt

BRETT AND I weren't the only ones battling colon cancer on campus. Jim, the husband of Heidi, the program coordinator for the Wheaton Center for Faith, Politics, and Economics, was facing a cancer similar to the one I'd weathered. Heidi and I emailed back and forth about Jim's cancer treatment issues even though we had never met. Dianne Smith, a slight woman in her mid-seventies with light gray hair, worked as an assistant to Wheaton's provost. Dianne had been diagnosed with colon cancer right around the time of my surgery.

The faculty banquet right before the fall semester was the first time I saw Dianne when I was well. I was so new to good health that the banquet was actually the first time I'd worn a tie in over a year. It felt like a pretty big deal.

I was talking to my friend Ward right before the start of the banquet when Dianne came over to say hello.

"Hi, how are you?" I asked, glad for the natural opportunity to connect.

We chatted about her treatments and how difficult they'd been.

"Jamie," she said in a quieter voice, "I'm so glad you're well. Our whole community prayed for you and God answered those prayers."

I thought I saw something in her face signaling that her mood was shifting.

"I'm so grateful for that," I said. I meant it.

Then she spoke what was really on her heart.

"Jamie," she queried, "I just don't understand."

I wasn't following.

"Understand what?"

"I don't understand why God heard our community's prayers for you," she explained, "and not for me."

Her tone was searching, earnest, kind. My shoulders fell forward as I exhaled. I could feel my eyes starting to well up. I didn't know what to say. The silence between us was filled with the chattering of fifty different conversations around the room. Seconds felt like an eternity as her honest and vulnerable question hung in the air between us.

Her innocent query cut to the heart of some of the most difficult questions about faith. *How does prayer work? Does God intervene? Does God not intervene?* They were questions with which I'd been wrestling, but I knew I didn't dare attempt to answer them.

"Dianne," I began, "I don't understand either."

The "why me?" I wrestled with when I was first diagnosed had been turned on its head. But I still wondered "why."

Why have I survived this life-threatening illness?

All I could do was open my arms to offer her a hug.

And with the quietest whisper of a voice I heard myself pipe, "I'm so sorry."

I was.

Her question would continue to haunt me.

Brett was also on my heart and mind. I always read his emails right away, but when I went to reply, my words kept getting hijacked on their way to my fingers. Wanting to find the right words, an internal voice would chide, *You owe him a more thoughtful response. Come back to it when you have time to write something meaningful.* On some level I knew I was avoiding responding, but I couldn't admit it to myself.

It was now early November, well over a year after Brett's diagnosis. I finally buckled down and took the time I needed to send a follow-up email to check in and share words of encouragement. I suggested it would be great to get together for coffee or a meal after I returned from an upcoming trip to Arizona and sent along some possible dates and times. I also apologized that I was going to miss a special production the Theater Department was performing, based on his written works, which Brett's friend Mark Lewis was directing. I shared how badly I wished I could have gone but had already committed to this trip before the special event had been announced.

I hit send on the email and quickly threw some belongings into my carry-on bag for a three-day trip to the Southwest. I was on my way to present at a mountaintop base camp, providing trauma training to a new group of humanitarian aid recruits who were preparing to join a relief and development organization headquartered in Switzerland.

The next morning, as I waited for the shuttle at the Phoenix airport that would drive me to the camp, I found myself tearing up after seeing one of Brett's poems that had been shared on Facebook describing his battle with cancer. It was as if each careful and painstaking word he chose captured experiences and emotions I had experienced during my own cancer journey but had not been able to articulate. Titled "Sad little patriarch, rubbing his gloved hands together," a piece of it reads,

> When will my own days feel real again,
> the frozen clock hands begin to turn again?
> When will this chemical burning in the veins
> stop, and hope, perhaps, be recompensed?
> I wear this long wool coat against the cold
> that hurts me, covered with two scarves,
> my face covered to avoid any feeling
> of cobwebs, with their every thread feeling
> like a tiny razor blade slicing the skin.
> There is no ounce of benignity in this feeling.

Regardless, I'd just been informed the previous week that I was eighteen months cancer-free I was hit hard by what I had just read.

Though physically I was sitting on a bench in a nearly empty corridor next to the baggage claim waiting for my ride, mentally I was jettisoned back to a small infusion room at the cancer center. I could smell the hospital-grade disinfectant. I could hear the soft yet piercing rhythmic beep from the monitor attached to my chemo drip. I remembered the way the needle felt as it punctured my skin and the port in my chest. I felt myself starting to brace for the icy shiver that always chased the medicine through my veins.

"Sir, sir, the shuttle is here," the woman behind the kiosk alerted me. I wiped my eyes, pulled myself together, gathered my belongings, and stumbled to the curb.

I boarded the small shuttle van to find two older male passengers inside, each sitting in a separate row, so I squeezed my way to the back row. As we began our journey to the mountains, they each engaged me in some small talk. I was grateful for the distraction. The man in the front slowly started falling asleep and eventually fell over and sprawled across the bench seat. Then the man in the second row started talking politics with the driver. Not wanting to be alone with my thoughts, I decided to distract myself with work. I'd had a busy week leading up to my flight, so I thought I would use my two-and-a-half-hour shuttle ride to prepare for my talk. I began mentally reviewing my main talking points, going back and forth with myself about trying out a new exercise that I hoped would get participants talking. Then I remembered I'd forgotten to integrate a couple of facts from an email I'd saved. As I was scanning email on my phone, my eyes fixed on one message's subject line from my employer: "A Colleague Has Passed." My friend Brett, the poet whose written words had come alive to me in the predawn hours at the airport, had died the night before. I was stunned and heartbroken by the news. It took a moment for what I had read to sink in.

Against my will, I once again found myself back in the boxing ring with cancer. My body's fight-or-flight response instinctively activated. Hunched over in my seat like a boxer anticipating an upper-cut punch to the face, I swung one hand to protect my face and cover my tears. But I couldn't stop the grief punch delivered to my stomach. The air was sucked out of my body. I wrapped my other arm around my abdomen to try and stop the shaking. My thoughts raced:

Why did this happen?

No, I must have misread it.

I don't understand.

Why him?

I just emailed; I didn't say good-bye.

No! No! No!

This could have been me.

This could have been my family, my wife, my daughters.

Why am I okay?

I think I'm going to throw up.

OH GOD—I FEEL SO GUILTY!

I took some deep breaths and hoped the only other two

conscious people on the shuttle hadn't noticed me falling apart.

Okay, Jamie. Okay, Jamie. Okay, Jamie, I said to myself as I tried to get a grip on my emotions.

I felt like I needed to turn around and go home.

How on earth am I going to give a training on trauma while I'm in the midst of my own?

Feeling completely helpless and alone, I was tortured by the thought that Brett and I had not shared our last meal together. I agonized that I was about to be wearing the hat of "trainer" when I wanted only for these aid workers to load me on a stretcher and send me straight home.

If I'd responded sooner . . .

If I'd carved out the time . . .

If I'd cancelled a meeting to meet with Brett . . .

Guilt and sadness mingled in the tears I shed on the shuttle bus to the training. I didn't know whether I'd be able to hold it together to teach that day.

Throughout my cancer journey I'd grown to understand that the professional and the personal could never be neatly separated. So rather than armor up and soldier through the trauma training as if I was not experiencing a trauma of my own, I let the class in on the struggle I was facing that day.

But despite my genuine effort at transparency, I couldn't bring myself to admit that I felt guilty for surviving.

In the wake of the crushing 2016 flood, our team deployed to the Baton Rouge area to provide disaster spiritual and emotional care training and conduct research. A common response we encountered among those whose homes were not devastated by winds and flooding—or not devastated as badly—was to feel "dry guilt." One person even described herself as having "minnow guilt"—minnow, as in a small freshwater fish. "How can I feel bad when I only had two feet of water in my home but my neighbor had six feet of water?" These more fortunate survivors felt as though they'd committed some sort of wrong for having fared well when so many had lost their homes. Dry guilt is one expression of a larger phenomenon called "survivor guilt." Originally identified in the 1960s among Holocaust survivors, those afflicted feel guilt for surviving what others have not: war, suicide, accidents, terrorism, and disease, among others. It can evoke feelings of helplessness, sadness, numbness, or shame. Survivors may withdraw from others, especially those who were affected. Survivor guilt had kept me from drawing closer to Brett, Heidi and her husband Jim, and Dianne. Knowing about survivor guilt, though, neither alerted me that I was experiencing it nor relieved it.

Brett's funeral was scheduled for the following Saturday. The morning of the funeral I gazed into the bathroom mirror as I fastened each button on my crisp white dress shirt. I'd been contacted by the *Washington Post* that week offering me an amazing writing opportunity. Tucking in my shirt, my mind turned to Brett's career. Brett had been such a gifted and prolific writer. Although he'd produced a lot of work already in his forty-two years, Brett had so much more to share. That I'd just gotten my first big writing break, and had enjoyed celebrating my daughter's eighth birthday the night before, hardly seemed fair.

Kelly's folks were in town for Chloe's birthday and were happy to watch the girls while Kelly and I ducked out for the 2 p.m. funeral. On the drive to Wheaton's Pierce Chapel, I remember feeling incredibly anxious. Panicky. When I lifted my hand to turn down the volume on the van radio, I noticed it shaking.

We entered the sanctuary, and I quickly chose a seat near the rear of the expansive room. I picked a spot near the outside edge, in case I had to make a quick getaway. Though I didn't have any other place I needed to be, I knew I didn't want to be where I was.

Was it possible that four hours earlier I'd been enjoying pancakes with my birthday girl in the kitchen? Kelly, Colleen, Carlee, and Chloe could just as easily have been sitting in that very first pew mourning *my* passing. But they weren't. That morning they'd been singing "Happy Birthday" and watching Disney videos. The absurdity of the polar extremes of our two families on that day stirred up a vortex of swirling chaos within me. Then, as quickly as it had come, it dissipated, leaving me crushed, with only sorrow and guilt.

The background music and small talk among those in attendance fell silent as the service started. Though I'm pretty sure I stood at the appropriate times, and even moved my mouth during songs, I felt almost catatonic throughout the service.

At the root of survivor guilt is a comparing of suffering.

No good can ever come from these kinds of comparisons, especially since we don't really know what another is experiencing.

Lives that look shiny and happy on Facebook can be riddled with dysfunction and pain. Others who may have a flair for the dramatic might always be moaning "woe is me" when the obstacles they face may not be as weighty as those faced by others. Even making that statement is problematic, since everyone responds to challenges differently! For example, studies have shown that comparing ourselves to others while using social media negatively affects well-being and increases feelings of loneliness and isolation. We found similar findings among Hurricane Matthew survivors, whose guilt came from comparing their disaster experiences to that of other survivors.

When we're aware of those comparisons, as I was when the CT scan technician let me know that my experience wasn't as bad as hers, we can react—quite appropriately!—with anger or sadness. But those kinds of comparisons are equally destructive when they're not vocalized. Though I'd never consciously compared what I endured as I battled cancer to what Brett, Dianne, or Heidi's husband had faced, the one comparison that mattered was undeniable: they were dead and I was alive.

I was afraid to approach their loved ones and even their friends and colleagues because I felt guilty about living. I feared my beating heart indicted me and might wound them even more. Though I knew intellectually that their suffering has no correlation to my survival, my gut bellowed otherwise.

Later that April, the Wheaton College Theater Department produced *The Sparrow*, a play exploring the aftermath of a tragedy in which a bus full of second-graders crashes into a train at a crossing. Protagonist Emily Book was the only survivor. As Emily's journey unfolds, it becomes evident that the community is shackled by pain and she is shackled by guilt.

Our friends Jared and Juliana had invited Kelly and me to join them for the play. As I watched I became aware that, like Emily, I was also shackled by guilt. All this time I thought I was struggling with sadness and anger. I even had passing moments where I was aware of my survivor guilt. However, up until that moment I had been like a homeowner investigating a crashing sound late at night from the porch, with a dim flashlight scanning the backyard. I could see the trashcans overturned but only caught a glimpse of something scurrying away under the cover of darkness. My sadness and anger, easy to make out, were like the obvious clanging noises. But the *source* of that sadness and anger was harder for me to see clearly—like the cat, raccoon, possum, or was it a small dog?—that had caused all the commotion. But after watching *The Sparrow*, I was finally able to both name and own my struggle with survivor guilt.

As we were leaving the theater, I caught a glimpse of Mark Lewis, Brett's friend who'd also orchestrated the production of Brett's poems around the time of his passing.

Catching Mark's attention, amid a horde of other well-wishers, I looked him in the eye.

"Mark, I know you loved Brett. He was a friend of mine, too."

Though the campus had rallied behind me, as it had for Brett, I didn't want to assume that Mark knew my whole story.

"Right when I found out I was healthy," I continued, "was when Brett was first in the hospital. And there were two other people connected to campus who also had a similar cancer around the same time."

His knowing eyes reflected kindness and compassion.

I articulated what the play had helped me to understand: "I lived; they did not." I added, "I thought maybe I've been battling anger, but now I see that it's survivor guilt."

With bold tenderness, he wrapped his arms around me and said, "Jamie, you have to keep living your story."

I received the words as a holy charge.

There are still moments when I experience pangs of guilt for continuing to live, and live well, when these other precious ones have not. And in those moments, I cling to the certainty that the abundant love and grace God had for each of them, in life and in death, are the same love and grace God has for me.

And whenever I notice those stabs of guilt, I recall Mark's charge: "You have to keep living your story."

I experienced an epiphany that night as I watched *The*

Sparrow, as I realized, for the first time, that I was living with more than sadness and posttraumatic symptoms. I was living with survivor guilt. Several months later, I would be given an opportunity to release that guilt.

Toward the beginning of the fall semester, three of my students planned to lead our class through an experiential exercise to introduce spiritual disciplines from the holiness tradition and had asked us all to meet at the Billy Graham Museum.

Parking in my usual lot, I dashed through the rain up the large stone steps to arrive just as the leaders ushered us into the museum. Feeling a bit raw, I was grateful to not be lecturing that day. The students organizing the class asked us to remove our shoes and leave them at the door. They offered us scarves to place over our heads as Christians had been instructed to do before entering the holiest of holiest places centuries earlier. Even typically playful or chatty students were embracing the reverent mood. We washed our hands in a small metal bowl near the doorway to a small private chapel. Inside the chapel the students led us in a brief time of worship, using some of the classic hymns of the church.

After the second hymn, one of the student leaders wove through the group handing out small sheets of paper and colorful pens, while another instructed us to write something that we could give to God. In lieu of the monetary offering common to Sunday morning worship services, we were being invited to release something else to God.

The student narrated, "It could be a destructive habit. A concern. Maybe an offense you haven't forgiven. Or one you've committed—"

Two words had landed in my heart before the student had finished speaking. She concluded, "Ask God what it is that you could release to him today."

Survivor guilt.

I knew the idea had been prompted by God's Spirit, but a part of me also knew that I wasn't yet ready to release it. Before I could change my mind, I quickly scribbled the two words in green ink. Then I jammed the paper in the left breast pocket of my blue coat. Although students were guiding the class, I was still the professor and didn't feel I had the leisure to indulge myself in personal self-reflection.

At the conclusion of the class, the students led us outside through two heavy wooden doors. I squinted my eyes as the dimness of the chapel gave way to the brightness outside. The rain and clouds had passed, and the sun was beaming brightly.

As our group circled up again, I pulled the crumpled paper from my pocket. As I glanced at the two words I knew God had given, my rote, dutiful words felt like a false offering. Like all of our personal defenses, the guilt I'd clung to had served a function.

The feelings of guilt I'd experienced had kept at bay that which I'd buried even more deeply: I had treated people dear to me like they had Ebola.

The unexpected insight gripped me with force. Without the guilt, I realized, I'd be forced to face my shame that came from feeling like I had treated Brett, Heidi and her husband, and Dianne similarly to how our fearful Ebola study participants had responded to Thomas Eric Duncan. I was afraid the pain, anger, and numbness toward God that I knew I harbored, but didn't want to admit, was lurking in the shadows of my shame. No wonder I wasn't willing to release the guilt. What its absence would reveal was even more terrifying to face.

Folding the paper into neat quarters, I put it back in my pocket.

I still believed that the words were from God.

But I knew I'd need time to release my grip. I understood in that moment that if I was going to trust God with my survivor guilt, I would also have to be willing to release to God the shame from which the guilt had been shielding me.

I had felt guilty for greedily grasping to life when my friends had not been as fortunate. With time I began to notice a sense of release from the weight of somehow feeling responsible for what had happened. It was as if God was methodically taking a spiritual hammer to my heart, chipping away at my survivors guilt. As those disparate pieces of truth sifted into my deep places, I was able to embrace that reality and release some of the guilt I'd been carrying.

CHAPTER 16

Surviving Survivorship

Living with Fortitude

I WAS SCROLLING THROUGH email on my laptop at the
cancer center's waiting room before seeing Dr. Patel,
but no mindless distraction could keep my mind from
worrying about the results I was about to receive from my
most recent CT scan. It had been almost three years since
I'd been given the "no evidence of disease" report. Still, I
knew how these sneaky diseases worked. Sometimes an
offending cell could hide away, perhaps for years, before
exploding into an army of militant attackers, intent on
destruction. Is that what Dr. Patel would tell me today?
Although I felt fine, I knew the possibility was real.

For those who've battled cancer, every anniversary is
a huge milestone. Each year I go without cancer coming
back, the better the odds I have of keeping cancer in my
past. So, if the cancer came back in less than five years,
I would be in serious trouble. My anxiety and stress had
peaked when I turned onto Diehl Road, an all-too-familiar
drive I was tired of taking. I parked my car in one of the last
open spots in the far corner of the parking lot. I was unable

to make myself unbuckle and get out of the car. I wanted to be anywhere other than there and do anything other than get my results. After turning off the engine I closed my eyes and leaned my car seat back a few inches. For five minutes I stayed reclined with eyes closed as I sang the words to one of my favorite hymns, "Amazing Grace," in my head. When I was receiving treatments, I discovered that focusing on the words of this spiritual classic right before getting my port accessed for drip chemotherapy had soothed me. I was hoping it would once again give me the strength I needed to unbuckle my seat belt, enter the hospital, and find a seat in the cancer center waiting room. I grabbed my backpack and headphones as I exited the car, thinking that distracting myself with some work and music might help.

I was so nervous about what might be found that I gave up on accomplishing writing or other real work and instead just focused on knocking out some email. A quick glance around the room, noticing and relating to what I saw in the eyes of others, stirred up feelings of fear I hadn't felt in a while. In fact, I had finally felt like I was starting to make progress. Though various unexpected challenges would emerge, I was enjoying time with my family and work was going well. Suddenly, though, I was scared that the life I treasured could all be snatched away in a heartbeat.

No sooner had I logged in to email than a message from someone I didn't know popped up at the top of my inbox. An organizer at the Fred Hutchinson Cancer Research Center in Seattle was inviting me to participate in an upcoming conference on survivorship at the center by giving the keynote talk. I quickly slammed shut my computer. I was caught off guard by the timing and topic of the email. I felt like such a phony. It had just taken me five minutes to be able to open my car door to exit my vehicle. I couldn't even bring myself to make eye contact with anyone else in the waiting room. *I'm the guy they want to come speak on survivorship?* The thought required me to fight back a rush of shame.

I'd recently attended the January conference at the Institute for Research on Psychology and Spirituality at Biola University. Prior to the trip, I had been researching virtues and character development because I'd started to wonder if there might be a biblical equivalent to the psychological concept of resilience. I'd begun to read more philosophy and theological writings, meeting with professors from these disciplines on campus, and I'd also started having Skype calls with experts in the United States and email correspondence with scholars at Oxford and Cambridge. While I had dedicated my career to studying faith and resilience, common definitions of resilience just didn't resonate with my personal experience of suffering. "Endurance" was the concept that came closest to identifying what I'd experienced and observed in others—but I couldn't shake the feeling there had to be a better nomenclature or model still out there.

In a passing conversation on a brief break, I shared this wrestling with my colleague Mark McMinn. He asked, "Jamie, have you looked into the virtues?" He was referring to the classic Christian virtues adopted by the church fathers: prudence, justice, temperance, courage, faith, hope, and charity. That's when it hit me. Another word used to name the virtue of courage is fortitude, and that felt like it might have a little more traction than "resilience" in trying to make sense of what I observed about my own experience and the experience of those I've studied after disasters. *Maybe this is exactly what I've been looking for.* As I began reading about these classic Christian virtues, all I was learning about "fortitude" struck me as being deeply true. Thomas Aquinas named fortitude as an act of "brave endurance."

Earlier in my journey, when I failed to experience the bouncy quality of resilience or the concept of endurance served me well. Yet when I discovered something even more robust, when I stumbled upon spiritual fortitude, it was as if a Rubik's Cube of all the lessons I'd learned had suddenly snapped into place. So endurance, my faithful traveling companion for a season, led me to a heartier experience of spiritual fortitude. Spiritual fortitude is what I had been searching for; I just hadn't known it at the time. For the first time I had the language I needed to understand what I had just been through and the words I needed to be able to share about my experience with others.

After I arrived at the airport to await my red-eye flight from Los Angeles to Chicago, I quickly Googled phrases like "biblical resilience" and "virtue of fortitude." By the time I boarded my plane I had about fifteen different Safari pages open and ready to read on the flight home.

"Mr. Aten?"

Dr. Patel's nurse stood at the door of the waiting room, inviting me to accompany her. Drawing a deep breath, I thrust my phone into my satchel, stood, and followed her back to a patient room. After the obligatory weighing and checking in, she left me to wait for the doctor.

Though tempted to lose myself in my phone again, I noticed the impulse and paused. I would wait undistracted, I decided, for whatever news Dr. Patel would deliver. Leaving my phone in the pocket of my bag, I opened my clenched hands and tipped raised palms toward heaven. Closing my eyes and taking another deep breath, I prayed quietly, placing my trust in the One who cared for me. Intrusive thoughts about not being able to grow old with Kelly or be around to see my girls grow up forced their way into my consciousness. I didn't try pushing back. I let them unfold. They evaporated almost as quickly as they had come on, giving way to a deep sense of God's loving-kindness to me and to my family.

When I heard the door handle jostle, I opened my eyes as Dr. Patel entered the room. Reaching to shake his outstretched hand, I fumbled grasping his palm. Like my feet, I was left with permanent nerve damage in my fingertips. Though I had regained most of the sensation in my fingertips, some lingering neuropathy remained. It had been a long time since I struggled to button my shirt, but occasionally made for awkward moments like dropping a drink, or in this case, an awkward handshake. I searched Dr. Patel's face for signs of what kind of news he was about to deliver.

As if reading my anxiety, Dr. Patel cut to the chase and offered, "Good news, Jamie. The CT scan was clear. We didn't see anything new."

I felt a rush of emotion well up behind my eyes.

"Thank you, doctor," I replied, filled with gratitude.

"We'll just keep checking," he reminded me. "But for now, just keep doing everything you've been doing to stay healthy."

We chatted for a bit, and then I left.

As I passed through the waiting room, I felt excited about the good news I had just received. But the extra step I had in my gait quickly dissipated as my prayers turned to the people I passed in the waiting room on my way out. Once I got back into my car, I texted Kelly the good news. I had made it another six months with no evidence of disease.

Filled with relief, I let my mind return to the invitation I'd just received. I noticed that I was energized as I thought about being able to share some of what I was learning, about fortitude in particular, with folks who were on journeys similar to my own.

As I'd been spending more time with the Christian virtues, I'd become convinced that fortitude was what I had been searching for. Though new to psychological science, fortitude is not a new concept. The church has long taught fortitude as the virtue of adversity and named it as one of the biblical fruits of the spirit (Gal. 5:22), marked by endurance and enterprise. According to the Diocese of La Crosse, "Endurance helps us to keep going when we are fatigued, suffering, weak, exhausted, or facing discouragement. Enterprise helps us to undertake great deeds while withstanding hardship." Within the Christian tradition, fortitude is commonly associated with pursuing good in the face of fear and hardship. It preserves us in times of overwhelming challenges. At the core of fortitude is the ability to cope with long-suffering. "Fortitude is the guard and support of other virtues," noted Enlightenment period English philosopher and physician John Locke. The concept captured my experience and the experience of so many survivors who didn't feel like popular definitions of resilience captured their experience.

The new way of thinking was taking root for me, to the point that our team joked they were going to have a T-shirt emblazoned with the phrase "Ask Me about Spiritual Fortitude." Darryl Van Tongeren and our other colleagues agreed to help me develop an empirical scale of spiritual fortitude. But the need for a fresh understanding wasn't rooted solely in my experience: data from several of our studies were pointing to a gap and need for further study, too. As a result, we were able to apply scientific language to identify what was happening in some survivors. And our preliminary scale development studies showed spiritual fortitude to be distinct from resilience and constructs like grit, which is "perseverance for long-term goals." Overall, spiritual fortitude helps people withstand adversity—especially when there is no clear end in sight—as they metabolize and lean into suffering.

And, of course, the new lens provided a fresh framework for me to look back and revisit my own journey. As I surveyed my experience and reactions during and after impact, well into the recovery and rebuilding phases, I was able to see differently through the perspective that fortitude afforded.

When I arrived at my office after my meeting with Dr. Patel, I reread the invitation from the Fred Hutchinson Cancer Research Center. Although it had seemed to have come from out of the blue, it wasn't entirely unrelated to other work I was doing. I had just started a new grant on Christian meaning-making, suffering, and the flourishing life. I'd been apprehensive about joining the project when my colleague Liz Hall had first invited me onboard, as this study of personal disasters had been my first professional scientific foray away from studying mass disasters. I'd been concerned the work would hit too close to home, but because I had benefited so much from the insights and overlap between the two worlds, I did want to make what I was learning available to others who were figuring out how to live in the wake of personal disaster.

After checking my calendar and talking with Kelly, I replied to the organizer at the Center with an enthusiastic yes. At least that's how it read. But behind my acceptance was still a lot of uncertainty and nervousness.

Am I ready for this? I worried, after hitting reply.

By this point I had given a couple of brief talks about my cancer disaster. As I continued to send a few more emails, the reality of what I had just agreed to do started to sink in:

I would be giving a full hourlong keynote address to other survivors and those still getting treatment.

Until this point in my journey, I had chosen to keep my colostomy private. A handful of family members and friends were aware of it. While I believed, intellectually, that there was nothing inherently shameful about the new reality—which had afforded me *survival!*—it still felt that way at times. If I was honest, I was very concerned about people in my community finding out about it. I feared that they'd look at me differently. When my bag leaked during a class, although no one was aware of it but me, I was mortified. I rushed out of the room at the end of class to dash home to change. The incident only confirmed that I much preferred to keep the bag, and all it represented, hidden out of sight.

As I prepared for the conference, though, I toyed with the possibility of mentioning my colostomy publicly for the first time. If there was ever an audience in front of whom I could be completely real, this was it.

I flew out to Seattle on a Friday night to deliver my talk on Saturday. After waking up in the hotel Saturday morning, I grabbed a quick breakfast and then headed to the conference. The auditorium was full, with about three hundred cancer survivors and caregivers in attendance. A few wheelchairs, a walker, a few prosthetic limbs, and a number of head scarves signaled what the disease had stolen from those gathered. Others who'd gathered had been disease-free for a year, or five, or ten. Each attendee understood that the impact of cancer on a patient—on a survivor—was more pervasive than physical symptoms and could not be measured only in blood counts and CT results. Wellness was more than physical health.

I was up first to kick off the event. As I approached the podium I breathed a quick prayer that my words would touch the hearts of those who'd come. I opened my mouth to speak, but no one beyond the first few rows could hear me. My wireless lapel mic wasn't working. After a few minutes of trying to fix it, the tech guy gave me a handheld one. I began my talk again by informing the group I talk a lot with my hands and jokingly apologized up front if I accidentally tossed the handheld mic into the crowd while speaking, warning them to stay sharp. I then asked how many Seattle Mariners fans were in attendance. Almost every hand shot straight up in the air.

As a die-hard Cubs fan, I jested, "If you all catch like the Mariners, then we might be in trouble."

When they jokingly jeered right back, I knew these were my sort of people.

When I speak, I have an outline or PowerPoint presentation in front of me, but I don't draft every word of my talk, and that way I can stay connected to those listening. When I teach my students, present academic research, and speak at conferences, I try to read the faces of those who've gathered and notice what catches their attention. This was one of the most engaged groups to whom I'd spoken. I could tell they were connecting with the personal stories I shared and also the new research we had begun to conduct on fortitude. I stepped out from behind the podium, where my outline rested, shortly after I started my talk. I never went back behind the podium, didn't use the PowerPoint, and never looked back at my notes.

As I unpacked my own story, I admitted the reticence I'd had ever since my surgery. I described how I still struggled with the way the surgery had changed my body. When I mentioned the zipperlike scars, I saw heads nodding in the audience.

"Even though I make jokes about how cancer has affected my body," I confessed, "I still struggle with how my body has changed, especially the fact that I had to have a colostomy."

As I heard the words escape my lips, I felt both the lightness of a weight being lifted and terror that I had just shared this with a room full of strangers. In my nervousness I quickly followed by disclosing this was the first time I had revealed this in public. My self-revelation was met not with the pitiful looks or disgusted glances I'd feared, but with *clapping*! This auditorium of people understood my vulnerability in sharing this piece of my story that I'd chosen to keep private until then.

After the talk, the conference organizer dismissed everyone for a day's worth of breakout sessions. As many flooded out, a group of attendees gathered near the stage to speak with me. I began to hear stories about surgeries, catheters, amputations, colostomies, and all manner of indignities that survivors had suffered. But as each one was revealed, I didn't hear shame or experience it. Instead of seeing irreparably wounded survivors in front of me, I saw victors who'd fought the good fight and survived their battles as well as those who were still bravely facing them.

After chatting with the final lingerers in the auditorium, I quietly migrated to the cafeteria to grab a coffee. I chose a seat hidden in the back to let what had happened sink in. Although I'd planned to attend and take advantage of the great breakout sessions scheduled for the day, that's not how my afternoon unfolded at all.

A young man in his early twenties who used a wheelchair settled in to the table next to mine, striking up a conversation. As we chatted, I learned that he'd had over forty surgeries, including several on his head and brain. A few more folks joined us, and they gifted us by sharing pieces of their stories. Every story was wildly unique. Each one involved a loss that had not been chosen. As some folks left, others joined us.

I noticed a buzz of vitality in my heart. Feeling connected to these survivors in ways I hadn't with many other people, I saw that something special was happening—as if we were speaking the same language and sharing a common understanding. Because the conversation was giving me life, as I suspected it was to others, I gave myself permission to visit a bit longer, to listen, and to be healed by their sharing. I stayed in the cafeteria connecting with people and listening to their stories until I had to depart for the airport. For over five hours *I just listened.*

And what I heard, from person after person, was the reality I'd been too slow to own: we are forever changed by what we've endured. Trying to hide our scars doesn't change the fact that we've been altered by our experience. I learned that we can let our wounds wall us off from others. Or we can use our wounds as doorways through which we invite others to enter and share our most true authentic self.

I met one woman at the conference who likened cancer survival to wearing a hoodie that you can never take off. Sometimes the hoodie covers your face with the drawstring pulled tight, making it hard to see anything. Sometimes the sleeves are stretched over your hands wrapped around you and tied like a straitjacket. Sometimes you can remove the hood and push up the sleeves past your elbows. Sometimes you wear the hoodie wrapped around your waist like it is hardly there at all. Whether in treatment or remission, the hoodie is always with you in one way or another. Her analogy captured for me, in such a helpful way, my experience of survivorship.

For research purposes, we defined *spiritual fortitude* as "enabling people to endure and make redemptive meaning from adversity through their sacred connections with God, others, and themselves." Following Hurricane Matthew, our team found that spiritual fortitude correlated with positive religious coping, experiencing meaning in life, and spiritual well-being. That is, we found support for the notion that spiritual fortitude helped survivors remain engaged in their faith rather than abandoning it. Specifically, spiritual fortitude facilitated positive religious coping—cultivating individuals' perceived relationship with a benevolent God—which in turn enhanced survivors' ability to find meaning and spiritual resilience in the wake of disaster.

Being in the presence of those fierce survivors at Fred Hutch woke me up to a reality about survivorship and fortitude that I may have known in a peripheral or intellectual way but that landed squarely in my heart that day. Although, like many, during my earliest days and weeks and months of survival I had chosen to hide my scars, I was discovering that there was actual healing and new life as I chose to expose them to light and air. If I had feared that revealing the nature of my woundedness would drive others from me, I was learning that just the opposite was true. Our points of vulnerability are precisely where we connect with others. And, somewhat counterintuitively, "brave endurance" meant tearing down walls of strength and protection, not building them. Walls of protection didn't give me life. Exposing my vulnerability in safe spaces did. Unlike military fortitude, the kind that armors up for battle, spiritual fortitude comes through embracing our weaknesses.

When I arrived home Saturday night after my journey from Seattle, I snuck into the house after midnight. Peeking into the girls' rooms, I noticed Chloe's blue rubber anklet resting in the glow of her nightlight, on her dresser. Seeing her remove it from her ankle, as if lifting death from her body and from our family, had been such a special moment for me. But that day I'd become keenly aware of the ways in which owning the full reality of what we endure—the wounds, the scars, the disfigurements, the disappointments, and even the small deaths we've weathered—is more honest and more *healing* than creating a reality that skirts the truest story about who we are and what we've been through.

As I slowly opened the door to the bedroom Kelly and I shared, mentally willing the door to be less loud and creaky than it actually was, I walked straight to my nightstand, opened the bottom drawer, and fished around under some books until I retrieved a blue rubber bracelet matching the one Chloe had saved. I quietly placed it in the front pocket of the backpack I carry everywhere as a reminder that life was different now but that there was no life in trying to hide my illness, my past, or my scars.

That bracelet, now always kept close in my backpack, reminds me daily of both what I weathered and also how much I still need community.

Postscript

ABOUT FOUR MONTHS after I'd completed my treatments, I'd been getting dressed for work on a Monday morning in front of the mirror in my room. I hadn't seen Carlee enter the room. Since she was a whirring ball of energy, the miss was a rarity. I saw her reflection in the mirror as she surveyed the scars the surgeon's knife had left on my chest and torso. I was caught off guard and wasn't sure how to respond. I was frozen by my self-consciousness as I saw her big brown eyes take in the railroad-like scar that ran up and down my abdomen. I felt worried about her seeing me this way. She also noticed the colostomy bag.

After a long pause she tenderly queried, "Daddy, will you have those scars and a pouch in heaven?"

Shortly after I had returned home from my first major surgery, Kelly and I had explained to our children how my body had been affected by the operations. "Daddy has new plumbing," we shared as we described the colostomy and scars and offered a brief glimpse at the pouch. After that I'd done my best to try and keep it hidden. And just as when we had first broken the news of my cancer diagnosis, we took time to answer questions and did our best to be honest with them. I had struggled to accept how my body had changed in this life, let alone considering what might be next.

"Well, Carlee," I said in a barely audible voice, "in heaven God will give Daddy a new body so I *won't* have any more pain or need my supplies anymore."

I could almost see the gears turning in her head as she processed my response. As my words began to take hold, a tiny smile started to form in the corner of her mouth that slowly grew large and joyful. The silence was finally broken when she threw a fist up in the air and pulled it down to her side—as if she'd just singlehandedly won the WNBA championship—and exclaimed, "Yes!"

My journey has convinced me that it's through our struggles—not our changed circumstances—that our hearts and minds are reconciled with what is while sustaining hope for what could be. Carlee's exuberant celebration reminded me of what is most true for all of us: God is faithful to redeem our disasters, be it in this life or the next.

Acknowledgments

I COULD NOT HAVE written *A Walking Disaster* without the help and support of so many. The people on this list have all helped to make this book come to life and encouraged me during a very difficult time in my life.

To Kelly Aten: Thank you for all the love and support you showed and gave me and our girls as we battled cancer. Thank you for being by my side every step of the way and for the sacrificial ways you took care of our girls and me and held our family together.

To Colleen, Chloe, and Carlee Aten: Thank you for the joy you have brought and continue to bring to my life. Each of you are so special to me and I'm fortunate to be your dad.

To my parents, Pam and Dean Aten: Thank you for your love as I faced cancer.

To my in-laws Bob and Karen Blunk: Thank you for all the ways you helped our family.

To all my family and friends, both near and far: Thank you for reaching out and finding ways to help and encourage me. I owe a special thanks to the community of Oblong where I first learned about faith and resilience.

To the entire Wheaton College community: Thank you for your grace and all the ways you ministered to my family and me.

To Ward Davis: Thank you for your friendship and all the times and ways you encouraged me and were there for me.

To Josh Hook: Thank you for the regular texts and calls to see how I was doing and for visiting when you were in town from Texas.

To David Entiwhistle: Thank you for your support and encouraging emails and conversations.

To Ward Davis, Josh Hook, Daryl Van Tongeren, Donnie Davis, Laura Shannonhouse, and Laura Captari: I'm grateful for all the research we've collaborated on and even more grateful for your friendship. And I want to point out anytime I use the word "we" when referring to research throughout this book I'm almost always talking about some combination of this incredible group of scholars and researchers.

To my Humanitarian Disaster Institute colleagues, Kent Annan, Jenny Hwang, Laura Leonard, Juana Trujillo, Jenn Hook, Rose Dickson, David Boan, and Katherine Anderson: Thank you for all the ways you have helped make the institute what it is today.

To Alice Schruba, Marianne Millen Carlson, Wendy Smith, Dan Martinson, Ben Andrews, Jordan Synder, Jessica Polson, Isaac Weaver, James Kent, Grace Spencer, Melissa

Smigelsky, Alison Gill, Deb Foshager, and the countless other students who have been a part of my research lab: I appreciate how you contributed to the projects highlighted in this book and helped while I was facing cancer.

To Sharon Topping, John Hosey, Roberta Avila, C. J. Caufield, Alice Graham, Beverly Wallace, William Livingston, Ryan Denney, Kari Leavell, Rose Chinn, Justin Defee, Tania Bayne, Anita Chandra, Joie Acosta, and all the other incredible people I had a chance to work alongside following Hurricane Katrina: I appreciate all the work you did to help others and for what I learned from you.

To Miranda Meadows: Thank you for being there for our girls during my cancer battle and connecting with them on everything from living in the South to art.

To Ekklesia, our Mississippi church family: Thank you for sending your support across numerous state lines; I still have the book of handwritten notes you sent.

To Renewal Church: The first time we walked through your doors was after the story I've shared in this book. Thank you for welcoming our family into your community and walking alongside us as we enter a new chapter of our cancer story.

To my mentors over the years, especially Mark Gallagher, Michele Boyer, Michael Shuff, Diann Bomer, David Hasty, and John Makosky: Thank you for shaping my path.

To my medical and health-care team: Thank you for the incredible care you have and continue to provide me.

To Susan Arellano, Angelina Horst, Trish Vergilio, Dan Reilly, and the whole Templeton Press team: Thank you for the opportunity to share my story and for all your incredible support throughout the entire publishing process.

To Margot Starbuck and Tim Morgan: I appreciate all the time, guidance, and mentorship you've invested in me as a writer and for teaching me how to translate statistics into stories.

To the John Templeton Foundation: Thank you for the generous support of our team's research and work.

To those who have or are journeying through personal, mass, or humanitarian disasters who shared your stories, encouragement, and wisdom with me personally or through my work: Thank you—and I pray what I have learned from you and have attempted to share in this book will give hope to others in the same way you have given me hope.

Notes

28: Our research on the survivors of the Liberian . . . Ochu, A. C., Davis, E. B., Magyar-Russell, G., O'Grady, K. A., & Aten, J. (2018). Religious coping, dispositional forgiveness, and posttraumatic outcomes in adult survivors of the Liberian civil war. *Spirituality in Clinical Practice, 5*(2), 104–19.

48: We now know, through emerging research . . . Schruba, A. N., Davis, E. B., Aten, J. D., Wang, D. C., Entwistle, D. N., & Boan, D. (2018). Psychological first aid and the role of scientific evidence in Christians' provision of disaster spiritual and emotional care. *Journal of Psychology and Christianity, 37,* 74–79.

57: Also a culture in which doing for one's self . . . http:/trudye bell.com/Bell-63: AidAmbivalence1913_text_HoltConf_3-25-09.php

58: I was afraid of having an experience similar . . . Leavell, K., Aten, J., & Boan, D. (2012). The lived coping experiences of South Mississippi and New Orleans Clergy affected by Hurricane Katrina: An exploratory study. *Journal of Psychology & Theology, 40,* 336–48.

63: The average age when people are diagnosed . . . https://www.ccalliance.org/get-information/what-is-colon-cancer/risk-factors/

68: But Picou discovered that those in the local community . . . Picou, J. S. (2009). When the solution becomes the problem: The impacts of adversarial litigation on survivors of the Exxon Valdez oil spill. *University of St. Thomas Law Journal, 7,* 68–88.

106: About a year after Hurricane Katrina, our team . . . Aten, J., & Boan, D. (2016). *Disaster Ministry Handbook.* Downers Grove, IL: InterVarsity Press.

113: My fellow collaborators and I had studied West Virginia's . . . Curtis, J. B., Aten, J. D., Smith, W., Davis, E. B., Hook, J. N., Davis, D. N., Von Tongeren, D. R., Shannonhouse, L, DeBlaere, C., Ranter, J., & Cuthbert, A. D. (2017). Collaboration between clergy and mental health professionals in disaster contexts: Lessons from the Upper Big Branch Mine disaster. *Spirituality in Clinical Practice, 4,* 193–204. doi:http://dx.doi.org/10.1037/scp0000129

127: Years later our team interviewed Congolese women . . . Smigelsky, M., Aten, J., Gerberich, S., Sanders, M., Post, R., Hook, K., Ku, A., & Boan, D. (2014). Trauma in Sub-Saharan Africa: Review of cost, estimation methods, and interventions. *International Journal of Emergency Mental Health, 16*(2), 354–65.

137: Years earlier I researched the benefits of spiritual surrender . . . Aten, J., Bennett, P. R., Hill, P. C., Davis, D. E., & Hook, J. (2012). Predictors of God concept and God control after Hurricane Katrina. *Psychology of Religion and Spirituality, 3,* 182–92.

162: To avoid disrupting the children's education . . . *"Kids pulled out of class over concerns about principal's trip to Zambia.".* WAPT.com. Retrieved October 19, 2014.

188: I'd been apprehensive about joining the project . . . Hall, M. E. L., Shannonhouse, L, Aten, J., McMartin, J., & Silverman, E. (2018). The varieties of redemptive experiences:

A qualitative study of meaning-making in evangelical Christian cancer patients. *Psychology of Religion and Spirituality.* Advance online publication. doi:http://dx.doi.org/10.1037/rel0000210

193: Following Hurricane Matthew, our team found that spiritual . . . McElroy-Heltzel, S. E., Van Tongeren, D. R., Gazaway, S., Ordaz, A., Davis, D. E., Hook, J. N., Davis, E. B., Aten, J. D., Shannonhouse, L. R., & Stargell, N. A. (2018). The role of spiritual fortitude and positive religious coping in meaning in life and spiritual well-being following Hurricane Matthew. *Journal of Psychology and Christianity, 37,* 17–27.

Recommended Reading

CHAPTER 1

Aten, J. (2012). More than research and ruble: How community research can change lives (including yours and your students). *Journal of Psychology and Christianity, 31,* 314–19.

Aten, J., Boan, D., Davis, E. B., & Schruba, A. N. (2018). The Humanitarian Disaster Institute: A training model for graduate-level psychology and counseling programs. *Journal of Psychology and Christianity, 37,* 80–86.

CHAPTER 2

Aten, J., Boan, D., Hosey, J., Topping, S., Graham, A., & Im, H. (2013). Building capacity for responding to disaster emotional and spiritual needs: A clergy, academic, and mental health partnership model (CAMP). *Psychological Trauma: Theory, Research, Practice, & Policy, 5,* 591–600.

Aten, J., O'Grady, K., Milstein, G., Boan, D., & Schruba, A. (2014). Spiritually oriented disaster psychology. *Spirituality in Clinical Practice, 1,* 20–28.

Winter, M. (2012, December 26). Overwhelmed Newtown asks public to stop sending gifts. *USA Today.* Retrieved from https://www.usatoday.com/story/news/nation/2012/12/26/newtown-sandy-hook-school-shooting-halt-gifts/1792553/

CHAPTER 3

Aten, J., Moore, M., Denney, R., Bayne, T., Stagg, A., Owens, A., Daniels, S., Boswell, S., Schenck, J., Adams, J., & Jones, C.

(2008). God images following Hurricane Katrina in South Mississippi: An exploratory study. *Journal of Psychology and Theology, 36,* 249–57.

Davis, E. B., Kimball, C. N., Aten, J., Andrews, B., Van Tongeren, D. R., Hook, J. N., Davis, D. E., Granqvist, P., & Park, C. L. (in press). Religious meaning making and attachment in a disaster context: A longitudinal qualitative study of flood survivors. *Journal of Positive Psychology.*

Leavell, K., Aten, J., & Boan, D. (2012). The lived coping experiences of South Mississippi and New Orleans clergy affected by Hurricane Katrina: An exploratory study. *Journal of Psychology & Theology, 40,* 336–48.

Wood, B., Worthington, E., Exline, J., Yali, A., Aten, J., & McMinn, M. (2010). A brief measure of anger and positive attitudes toward God: Psychometric development, refinement, and validation of the attitudes toward God. *Psychology, Religion, and Spirituality, 2,* 148–67.

CHAPTER 4

Aten, J., Leavell, K., Gonzalez, R., Luke, T., Defee, J., & Harrison, K. (2011). Everyday technology for extraordinary circumstances: Possibilities for enhancing disaster communication. *Psychological Trauma: Theory, Research, Practice, & Policy, 3,* 16–20.

Aten, J., & Topping, S. (2010). An online social networking disaster preparedness tool for faith communities. *Psychological Trauma: Theory, Research, Practice, and Policy, 2,* 130–34.

CHAPTER 5

Aten, J., & Davis, E. B. (2018, June). The role of humility in resilient leaders (and communities). Plenary talk presented at the Robert Wood Johnson Foundation Integrative Action for Resilience Initiative, Princeton, NJ.

Boan, D., Andrews, B., Lowewer, E., Drake, K., Aten, J. (in press). A qualitative study of an indigenous faith-based distributive justice program. *Christian Journal of Global Health.*

Hook, J., Boan, D., Davis, D., Aten, J., Ruiz, J., & Maryon, T. (2016). Cultural humility and hospital safety culture. *Journal of Clinical Psychology in Medical Settings, 23*(4), 1–8. doi:10.1007/s10880-016-9471-x

Rodriguez, D., Hook, J. N., Farrell, J., Mosher, D., Zhang, H., Van Tongeren, D., Davis, D., Aten, J., & Hill, P. (2017). Religious intellectual humility, attitude change, and closeness following religious disagreement. *The Journal of Positive Psychology.* doi:10.1080/17439760.2017.1388429

CHAPTER 6

Dispenza, F., Davis, E. B., McElroy, S. E., Davis, D. E., Zeligman, M. R., Aten, J. D., Hwang, J., Van Tongeren, D. R., & Hook, J. N. (in press). Religious factors and global meaning violation in Louisiana flood survivors. *Traumatology.* Advance online publication. http://dx.doi.org/10.1037/trm0000166

Entwistle, D. N., Moroney, S. K., & Aten, J. (2018). Integrative reflections on disasters, suffering, and the practice of spiritual and emotional care. *Journal of Psychology and Theology, 46*, 67–81. doi:https://doi.org/10.1177/0091647117750658

Hall, M. E. L., Shannonhouse, L., Aten, J., McMartin, J., & Silverman, E. J. (2018). Religion-specific resources for meaning-making from suffering: Defining the territory. *Mental Health, Religion, & Culture.* doi:10.1080/13674676.2018.1448770

Haynes, W. C., Van Tongeren, D. R., Aten, J. D., Davis, E. B., Davis, D. E., Hook, J. N., Boan, D., & Johnson, T. (2017). The meaning as a buffer hypothesis: Spiritual meaning attenuates the effect of disaster-related resource loss on posttraumatic stress. *Psychology of Religion and Spirituality, 9*, 446–53. doi:dx.doi.org/10.1037/rel0000098

Wang, D. C., Aten, J. D., Boan, D., Wismick, J-C., Griff, K. P., Valcin, V. C., Davis, E. B., Hook, J. N., Davis, D. E., Van Tongeren, D. R., Abouezzeddine, T., Sklar, Q., & Wang, A. (2016). Culturally adapted spiritually oriented trauma-focused cognitive-behavioral therapy for child survivors of Restavek. *Spirituality in Clinical Practice, 3*(4), 224–36. doi:http://dx.doi.org/10.1037/scp0000101

Van Tongeren, D. R., Aten, J. D., Davis, E. B., Davis, D. E., & Hook, J. N. (in press). Religion, spirituality, and meaning in the wake of disasters. In S. E. Schulenberg (Ed.), *Disaster mental health and positive psychology.* New York, NY: Springer.

Van Tongeren, D. R., Sanders, M., Edwards, M., Davis, E. B., Aten, J., Ranter, J. M., Tsarouhis, A., Short, A., Cuthbert, A., Hook, J. N., & Davis, D. E. (2018). Religious/spiritual struggles alter God representations. *Psychology of Religion and Spirituality.* Advance online publication. doi:http://dx.doi.org/10.1037/rel0000173

CHAPTER 7

Liang, L., Hayashi, K., Bennett, P., Johnson, T., & Aten, J. (2015). Resource loss and depressive symptoms following Hurricane Katrina: A principal component regression study. *International Journal of Behavioral Research & Psychology, 3*, 91–98.

McElroy-Heltzel, S. E., Davis, E. B., Davis, D. E., Aten, J., Hook, J. N., Van Tongeren, D. R., & Hwang, J. (2018). Benevolent theodicies protect against PTSD following a natural disaster. *Journal of Psychology and Christianity, 37*, 6–16.

Chapter 8

Aten, J., Gonzalez, R., Boan, D., Topping, S., Livingston, W., & Hosey, J. (2012). Church attendee help seeking behavior in Mississippi and Louisiana following Hurricane Katrina. *International Journal of Emergency Mental Health, 14*, 15-20.

Davis, E. B., & Aten, J. D. (Eds.). (2018). Disasters, religion, and spirituality [Special issue]. *Journal of Psychology and Christianity, 37*(1).

CHAPTER 8

Aten, J., & Schruba, A. (2016). An integrative approach to hope, healing, and acceptance [Review of the book *Faith-based*

ACT for Christian clients: An integrative treatment approach, by J. J. Knabb]. *PsycCRITIQUES, 61*(49). doi:http://dx.doi.org/10.1037/a0040595

Beck, A. T., Steer, R.A., & Garbin, M.G. (1988) Psychometric properties of the Beck Depression Inventory: Twenty-five years of evaluation. *Clinical Psychology Review,* 8(1), 77–100.

Schruba, A. N., Aten, J. D., Davis, E. B., & Shannonhouse, L. R. (2018). A grounded theory of the practice of disaster spiritual and emotional care: The central role of practical presence. *Journal of Psychology and Christianity, 37,* 57–73.

Schruba, A. N., Davis, E. B., Aten, J. D., Wang, D. C., Entwistle, D. N., & Boan, D. (2018). Psychological first aid and the role of scientific evidence in Christians' provision of disaster spiritual and emotional care. *Journal of Psychology and Christianity, 37,* 74–79.

CHAPTER 11

Captari, L. E., Hook, J. N., Mosher, D. K., Boan, D., Aten, J. D., Davis, E. B., Davis, D. E., & Van Tongeren, D. R. (2018). Negative religious coping and burnout among national humanitarian aid workers following Typhoon Haiyan. *Journal of Psychology and Christianity, 37,* 28–42.

Smigelsky, M. A., Gill, A. R., Foshager, D., Aten, J. D., & Im, H. (2017). "My heart is in His hands": The lived spiritual experiences of Congolese refugee women survivors of sexual violence. *Journal of Prevention & Intervention in the Community, 45,* 261–73.

CHAPTER 13

Aten, J., & Walker, D. (Ed.). (2012, Winter). Special volume on religion, spirituality, and trauma. *Journal of Psychology and Theology.*

Massengale, M., Davis, D., DeBlaere, C., Zelaya, D., Shannonhouse, L., Van Tongeren, D., Hook, J., Aten, J., & Hill, P. (2017). Attachment avoidance to God exacerbates the negative effect of tangible resource loss on psychological resource loss. *Mental Health, Religion & Culture, 20,* 489–501. doi:10.1080/13674676.2017.1359242

Shannonhouse, L., Myers, J., Barden, S., Clarke, P., Weimann, R., Forti, A., Moore-Painter, T., Knutson, T., & Porter, M. (2013). Finding your new normal: Outcomes of a wellness-oriented psychoeducational support group for cancer survivors. *Journal for Specialists in Group Work, 39*(1), 3–28.

Walker, D., Curtois, C., & Aten, J. (2015). (Eds.). *Spiritually oriented trauma psychotherapy.* Washington, DC: American Psychological Books.

CHAPTER 14

Van Tongeren, D. R., Hook, J. N., Davis, D. E., Aten, J., & Davis, E. B. (2016). Ebola as an existential threat? Experimentally primed Ebola reminders intensify national-security concerns among extrinsically religious individuals. *Journal of Psychology and Theology, 44,* 133–41.

CHAPTER 15

Aten, J., & Boan, D. (2016). *Disaster ministry handbook.* Downers Grove, IL: InterVarsity Press.

CHAPTER 16

Cook, S., Aten, J., Moore, M., Hook, J., & Davis, D. (2013). Resource loss, religiousness, health, and posttraumatic growth following Hurricane Katrina. *Mental Health, Religion & Culture, 16,* 352–66.

Denney, R., Aten, J., & Leavell, K. (2010). Post-traumatic spiritual growth among cancer survivors. *Mental Health, Religion, and Culture, 13,* 1–21.

Van Tongeren, D. R., Aten, J. D., McElroy, S. Davis, D. E., Shannonhouse, L., Davis, E. B., & Hook, J. N. (submitted for review). Development and validation of a measure of spiritual fortitude.